SOCKS

A *Spin·Off* special publication
for knitters and spinners

edited by

Rita Buchanan and Deborah Robson

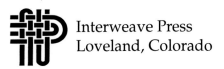
Interweave Press
Loveland, Colorado

Thanks to the following people for testing patterns: Rita Buchanan, Ann Budd, Teresa Gaffey, Donann Remund, Deborah Robson, Laura Sawyer, Jean Scorgie, and Susan Strawn. Any errors that appear were caused by mischievous electronic impulses. If you find an error, please drop us a postcard.

©1994, Interweave Press
All rights reserved
Library of Congress Catalog Number 93-47978
ISBN 0-934026-94-7

 Interweave Press
201 East 4th Street
Loveland, Colorado 80537

Library of Congress Cataloging-in-Publication Data
Socks: a Spin-off special publication for knitters and spinners /
   edited by Rita Buchanan and Deborah Robson.
       p.   cm.
   Includes index.
   ISBN 0-934026-94-7
   1. Socks.   2. Knitting—Patterns.   I. Buchanan, Rita.
II. Robson, Deborah.   III. Spin-off (Loveland, Colo.)
TT825.S66   1994
746.9'2—dc20   93-47978
                                                      CIP

The socks in this collection were designed by readers of Spin·Off *magazine.*

First printing: 10M:1293:HP/CL
Second printing: 10M:794:HP
Third printing: 7.5M:1295:HP
Fourth printing: 5M:797:HP
Fifth printing: 2M:299:VG
Sixth printing: 3M:1299:VG

Contents

Introductions 4
Yarn, equipment, difficulty, and sizing 5

Entrelac Socks *by Kathryn Alexander* 7
Lacy Arrow-patterned Socks *by Jean Sherman* 11
Double-knit Socks *by Jean Wright* 13
Turkish Stockings *by Ellen Dolson* 15

Techniques and abbreviations 17

Double-knit Socks *by Val Slemko* 20
Heavy Socks *by Irene Macrae* 22
Fleece-lined Socks *by Hannelore Krieger* 23
"Girly Girl" Socks *by Robin Fouquette* 26
Cabled Sweat Socks *by Claire Ottman* 29
Spiral Rib Socks *by Garry Aney* 30
Hound's-tooth Socks *by Marty Rather* 33
Fair Isle Socks for Clogs or Sandals *by Margaret Jaeger* 35
Hiking Boot Socks *by Margaret Jaeger* 38
Fundamental Socks *by Jude Daurelle* 39

Summary of yarns and gauges 41

Three-color Knee Socks *by Barbara Evans* 42
Hot Sox *by Susan Atkins* 44
Fireside Socks *by Joan Gooth-Buchanan* 47
Blue-and-white Socks *by Wilma Dibelka* 48
Very Basic Socks *by Ruth Blazenko* 51
Christmas Stocking Ornament *by Mary Spanos* 53

Bibliography and suppliers 55
Index 56

Introductions

The seed for this book was planted in the Fall 1991 issue of *Spin·Off* magazine, when we invited readers to "show us your socks." Soon the packages started arriving, filled with socks of all kinds—humble work socks, playful bed socks, thick woolly socks, delicate silky socks, plain white socks, multicolor socks, and complex patterned socks. We received over 160 pairs of socks from over 100 spinners across the United States and around the world. Along with the socks came yarn samples, patterns, tips, ideas, and stories. In the end, that little seed yielded a double harvest: a special feature for the Winter 1992 issue of *Spin·Off,* and this book of patterns.

I was the lucky editor who got to open the packages, read the letters, sort the socks, and organize the material for publication. It was a fascinating task, filled with discoveries and rich with emotions. Again and again, as I handled those socks, I was touched by the care, thought, patience, and persistence that went into the spinning and knitting, and the joy, pride, and fulfillment that came out. A pair of socks may be a small project in terms of time and yarn, but it's big enough to offer plenty of challenges and satisfactions.

Enthusiasm is contagious. It began with our contributors. Then we editors started knitting. Now it's your turn. Just one caution: once you start making socks, you may not be able to stop. I know one spinner who already has more than thirty pairs—different socks for every day of the month!—and the last time I saw her, she was knitting again.

Rita

Rita Buchanan
co-editor

Have you ever worn a pair of handknit socks? How about *handspun,* handknit socks? I hadn't, before *Spin·Off* magazine started exploring the world of socks. During twenty-five years of knitting, and almost as many of spinning, I had never been motivated to knit a sock.

When I slipped on the first sock I had knitted myself, I discovered there was no looking back. Made of a lovely commercial yarn, it gave me a sense of accomplishment disproportionate to the labor invested, the amount of yarn consumed, and the lack of star billing in my wardrobe.

I imagined how much finer the experience would be in a sock of my own handspun yarn—and it was!

Even the most complex of these patterns is suitable for "pick-up" knitting. A very small bag contains the yarn, equipment, and supplies. Fragments of time quickly add up to completed rows—it's not far around a foot. Socks are the perfect project for travel, soccer games, staff meetings.

Slip a finished pair on—and become aware that your *feet* are actually the part of your own body where you can wear special knitting and *see* it most often. And you wouldn't believe how good socks can feel. . . .

Most people, like me, have taken socks for granted. No more!

Deb

Deborah Robson
co-editor

Yarn

Because these socks were all designed and made with handspun yarn, the sizes of yarn may not precisely correspond to commercial weights . . . but then again, there's a range of options within each of the "standard" commercial designations, too. While we're particularly fond of handspun yarns, we knitted many of these patterns in commercial yarns in order to provide you with some guidelines. Our notes indicate the type of yarn to look for, and, when appropriate, the kind of yarn we used for our test.

Make a gauge swatch—that's crucial. While the gauge suggestions on yarn wrappers can be helpful, you'll find that many yarns can be knitted more tightly for socks than is acceptable for sweaters (the usual reference point). If you can achieve the appropriate gauge and like the feel and look of the fabric, you've found a good yarn.

Quantities are harder to specify. In sportweight yarn, ankle length socks require about 4 ounces (110 g). There's always some left over—a number of these patterns use small quantities of yarn for patterning. At the end of a sock-knitting spree, you may make some charmers from your surplus bits. In heavier weights of yarn, you'll need a larger quantity (by weight)—perhaps 6 ounces (170 g) in ankle length. For knee socks, you'll need about twice as much as for ankle length socks. The staff in good knitting shops can help you figure quantities for the yarns they supply, based on our guidelines and their own experience.

Equipment

Gauge is everything, and you can never have too many knitting needles. . . . The basic tool for making socks is a set of double-pointed needles. You'll need them for the toes, at least, and can knit from start to finish on them. Stores which understand devoted knitters also stock 11-inch (28-cm) circular needles, which can often be used for everything *but* the toes.

You'll always need a blunt tapestry needle, for grafting the small number of stitches which remain after the toes have been finished.

Although these are the essentials, a small, zippered "pencil" pouch stocked with a knitter's gauge (for checking needle sizes and measuring gauge swatches), ring markers, small scissors, stitch holders, and cable needles can be handy. Although Deb's is only 4 by 8 inches, it also holds extra sets of 7-inch (18-cm) double-pointed needles.

Difficulty

The patterns here range from extremely simple to quite challenging. If you're a beginner, start with the spiral rib socks (page 30), the fireside socks (page 47), or the heavy-winter toasty-toes socks (page 22). Then branch out into cables, color patterns, lace, or super-warmers (fleece-lined and double-knit).

Sizing, or "adult medium"

Feet are completely individual, and socks need to be, too. The biggest variation in size—the length of the foot—is also the easiest to fix. Most of the instructions tell you to knit until a certain number of inches less than the foot length before shaping the toe.

Socks with ribbing on the legs stretch more, and therefore fit different feet more easily than those with stockinette legs. The higher a sock comes on the leg, the more attention needs to be paid to the fit. The easiest socks in this book to fit: the spiral ribs, on page 30. The hardest: the knee socks on pages 35 and 42.

A number of our testers knitted socks to fit their large, or extra-large, feet. We've made notes on some of the patterns about how they altered the gauge, repeats, or yarn to change the size. If you have fitting questions, check our notes.

Any sock has to stretch enough to slide past the ankle and heel—this is usually the largest expanse that has to be negotiated. Rita has a nifty trick for checking fit. Cast on smallest number of stitches in the circumference of the sock, as the pattern is written; this is usually the number of stitches at the ankle. Knit about 3 inches (7.5 cm), using the appropriate pattern. Take the stitches off the needle, holding them on scrap yarn, and see if you can get the test section over your heel. If not, try another test on larger needles. By changing needles and thus making a minor adjustment in the gauge, you should be able to solve the problem and knit the pattern as written.

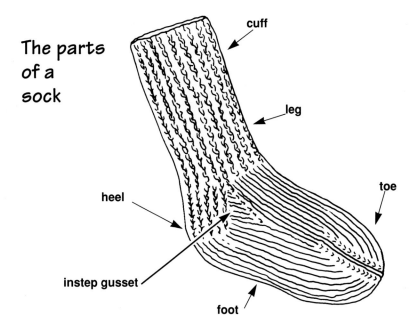

The parts of a sock

cuff

leg

toe

heel

instep gusset

foot

5

Although color isn't everything in these socks (you *could* make a single-color pair), there's lots of room to play. Kathryn Alexander and her mother accepted the challenge posed by a pair of Tibetan socks and figured out how to make the magic happen. The fine gauge is important to the effect, but the socks knit up quickly because they're so much fun.

Featured on the cover of the Winter 1992 issue of *Spin·Off,* Kathryn Alexander's entrelac socks caused an uproar in the community of knitters and spinners. Inspired by a pair of Tibetan socks brought to a workshop on designer yarns by spinner/teacher Diane Varney, Kathryn and her mother raced to figure out the secret of their construction. With clues from *Mon Tricot's 1300 Pattern Stitches* (1981), *Vogue Knitting* for Winter 1991–'92, and *Knitter's* for Summer 1992, they worked by trial and error until they mastered the form. Now it's your turn.

The socks shown here are a different pair than those we showed in the magazine, worked from the same concept in more muted colors. The pattern lends itself to color and design experiments. The spinning is a snap, because each complete row of squares requires only 12 yards—perfect for those short lengths of yarn that spinners always have. Kathryn says, "The socks became addictive, because there was no end to the design possibilities." Kathryn's instructions call for a fairly fine yarn, which produces delicate entrelac sections on versatile, not-too-heavy socks.

Entrelac Socks

Kathryn Alexander
Berkeley, California

←yarn sample
(actual size)

Size: Women's medium.
Yarn: Six colors of *fingering to laceweight yarn* at between 15 and 18 wraps/inch and approximately 106 yards per ounce. Kathryn used three-ply handspun yarns.

These socks are excellent for using small amounts of compatible yarns. Kathryn used a different color for each of the five rows of entrelac; the sixth color is the main color (MC). She cast on with the main color, knitted the first and last sets of triangles with it, carried it through the foot of the sock, and ended with it in the toe.

Precise color instructions are not given. Randomness is part of the charm of these socks, and the two members of a pair need not match exactly.
Needles: Double-pointed needles in sizes 1 (2.5 mm) and 2 (2.75–3 mm), or sizes needed to achieve correct gauge. Instructions are written for the use of five needles; if you are using four needles, you will need to count carefully, and perhaps use stitch markers, on the instep, foot, and toe.
Gauge: With larger needles in color patterns, 8–8⅓ sts = 1 inch (2.5 cm).

Cuff and leg. With larger needles and MC, cast on 52 sts. Distribute evenly on 4 needles and join. Work 1 round in k 2, p 2 ribbing, then change to smaller needles and continue in ribbing for 2 inches (5 cm), adding stripes and weaving in tails as you go.

Knit 1 round, decreasing 10 sts evenly (42 sts remain). Knit 2 rounds even.

Entrelac. On your first pair or two of these socks, you will probably want to turn your work as you build up the triangles and squares. However, Kathryn has adapted her technique for speed. To avoid constant turning of the work in the entrelac sections, she knits and purls backwards when appropriate. Instructions for modifying the pattern for speed will be contained in footnotes.[1]

First set of triangles.[2] Each triangle is worked back and forth on a set of 6

sts. Turn work at end of each row, except row 9. There are 7 triangles in the circumference of the stocking. *Row 1:* With right side of work facing and MC, k 2. *Row 2:* Sl 1 st purlwise, p 1 (these are the same 2 sts you worked in row 1). *Row 3:* K 3 (the same 2 sts, plus 1 more; this pattern continues, adding 1 st each time). *Row 4:* Sl 1 st purlwise, p 2. *Row 5:* K 4. *Row 6:* Sl 1 st purlwise, p 3. *Row 7:* K 5. *Row 8:* Sl 1 st purlwise, p 4. *Row 9:* K 6.

Repeat these 9 rows around, ending with seven 6-stitch triangles. You'll need to watch the placement of the completed triangles, so they don't all end up on one needle. Rotate as necessary.

Entrelac squares, set 1.[3] With wrong side facing and new color, pick up 5 sts purlwise along side of first triangle, working from tip to base; p 1 st from adjacent triangle on left needle (this st

---

[1] *To purl backwards:* With wrong side of work facing, insert needle as if to purl, and wrap yarn around. Turn work so right side is facing, noting where and how the needle and yarn are positioned. Continue to purl from the knit side. *To knit backwards:* With right side facing, insert needle and wrap yarn around as if to knit. Turn work so wrong side faces, noting where and how the needle and yarn are positioned. Continue to knit from purl side.

[2] In these triangles, purl backwards.

[3] For set 1, pick up purlwise, and knit backwards.

will be a different color). *Row 1:* K 6. *Row 2:* P 5, p 2 tog, again consuming 1 st from lefthand needle triangle. Repeat these 2 rows until all 6 sts from adjacent lefthand needle triangle have been consumed and the first square is complete. Work along the following triangles in same manner, creating entrelac squares as you knit.

Entrelac squares, set 2.[4] With right side of work facing and new color, pick up 6 sts along side of square, starting at its tip. Knit 1 st from lefthand needle, pass previous knit st over this. Again you will be consuming the sts from lefthand needle. *Row 1:* P 6. *Row 2:* K 5, sl 1, k 1 from lefthand needle, psso. Repeat these 2 rows until all sts from lefthand needle have been consumed.

Alternate rounds of squares in sets 1 and 2 until all squares are made, ending with set 1. Kathryn put five rows of entrelac squares in these socks.

Last set of triangles.[5] Begin these where you cast on, using cast-on yarn to mark center back. With right side of work facing and MC, pick up 5 sts knitwise starting at the tip of a square, k 1 from lefthand needle (this st will be a different color). *Row 1:* Sl 1 purlwise, p 1. *Row 2:* Sl 1 knitwise, k 2. *Row 3:* Sl 1 purlwise, p 3. *Row 4:* Sl 1 knitwise, k 4. *Row 5:* Sl 1 purlwise, p 5. *Row 6:* Sl 1 knitwise, k 6. *Row 7:* Sl 1 purlwise, p 6, p 2 tog. *Row 8:* Sl 1 knitwise, k 6, sl 1, k 2 tog, psso.

Continue in this manner until all spaces between entrelac squares have been filled in with 8-st triangles. Now 56 sts remain. Decrease 4 sts evenly (52 sts). With the sts divided evenly on four needles, there will be 13 sts on each one.

Change to larger needles and knit 2 rounds even. Begin working color designs. Kathryn uses combinations of 4-st patterns (k 2 first color, k 2 second color) and 2-st patterns (k 1 first color, k 1 second color), changing colors as

desired. A chart containing some possibilities is included here, but working freehand is a lot of the fun. Work for 1–2 inches (2.5–5 cm), depending on how much length is desired between entrelac pattern and beginning of heel flap, adding designs and changing color along the way. (In this sock, Kathryn knitted 1 inch or 2.5 cm.)

Heel. Place half the sts on one needle for heel flap (26 sts). With right side facing, knit across, knitting last 2 sts tog (25 sts), turn. Work first 4 sts in seed st; purl across to last 4 sts, alternating two colors to make vertical stripes; then work last 4 sts in seed st, turn. On next row, work 4 seed st, *sl 1 purlwise, k 1, * repeat from * to * across, weaving in slipped color across to last 4 sts; work 4 sts in seed st, turn. Repeat these two rows in pattern as established until heel flap measures 2½ inches (6.25 cm).

Next turn heel. With new color and right side facing, k first 2 sts tog, k remaining sts across (24 sts), turn. *Row 1:* Sl 1, purl across, turn. *Row 2:* Knit to 2 sts past center (14 sts), sl 1, k 1, psso, k 1.[6] *Row 3:* P 6, p 2 tog, p 1. *Row 4:* K 7, sl 1, k 1, psso, k 1. *Row 5:* P 8, p 2 tog, p1. *Row 6:* K 9, sl 1, k 1, psso, k 1. *Row 7:* P 10, p 2 tog, p 1. *Row 8:* K 11, sl 1, k 1, psso, k 1. *Row 9:* P 12, p 2 tog, p 1. *Row 10:* K 13, sl 1, k 1, psso, k 1. *Row 11:* P 13, p 2 tog. *Row 12:* K 14.

Instep and foot. With right side facing, place heel sts on two needles, evenly divided. Start at back of heel with new color. On needle 1, knit 7 sts of heel, then pick up and knit 12 sts along adjacent edge of heel flap. Knit across instep sts, dividing them evenly on needles 2 and 3. On needle 4, pick up and knit 12 sts along next adjacent edge of heel flap, then knit 7 remaining sts of heel. On next round and *every other round*, decrease as follows. At end

Possible color pattern chart (12 stitches wide):

```
●●●●●●●●●●●●
●●●●●●●●●●●●
XXXXXXXXXXXX
●●●●●●●●●●●●

●●●●●●●●●●●●



OOOOOOOOOOOO

 O  O  O  O  O  O
XOXOXOXOXOXO
XXXXXXXXXXXX

●●●VVVV●●●●
●●●VVVV●●●●
●●●VVVV●●●●
●●●VVVV●●●●
VVVV●●●●VVVV
VVVV●●●●VVVV
VVVV●●●●VVVV
VVVV●●●●VVVV
●●●●    ●●●●
●●●●    ●●●●

  /   /   /   /
 /   /   /   /
/   /   /   /
/   /   /   /
  /   /   /   /
   /   /   /   /

●O●O●O●O●O●O
●O●O●O●O●O●O
VVVVVVVVVVVV
VVVVVVVVVVVV
●●●●●●●●●●●●
●●●●●●●●●●●●

●●●●●●●●●●●●
XXXXXXXXXXXX
●●●●●●●●●●●●
```

← Possible color patterns for use in the stockinette areas of the entrelac socks. Assign your available colors to the symbols and experiment.

[4] For set 2, pick up knitwise, and purl backwards.

[5] Purl backwards.

[6] Begin purling backwards from here.

of needle 1, knit to last 3 sts, k 2 tog, k 1. Knit across instep sts. At beginning of needle 4, sl 1, k 1, psso. Continue in this manner until needles 1 and 4 are back to 13 sts each, for a total of 52 sts.

Knit foot of sock even in any color design, weaving in ends as you go, until sock is 2 inches (5 cm) less than desired length. Kathryn also puts color designs in the instep area, but on your first socks you will probably want to pay attention to the shaping alone in that area, beginning your color work on the straight section of the foot.

Toe. Begin toe decreases. On needle 1, knit to last 3 sts, k 2 tog, k 1. On needle 2, sl 1, k 1, psso. Knit across to last 3 sts of needle 3 and k 2 tog, k 1. On needle 4, sl 1, k 1, psso. Knit to end of needle. Work 1 round even. Repeat these 2 rounds until 6 sts remain on each needle (24 sts total). Place 12 sts on one needle for top of toe and 12 sts on another needle for sole. Graft together.

Kathryn began spinning in 1984, and in 1986 started her own business, Creekside Fibers. She raised Angora rabbits and llamas, sold yarns and fibers, gave spinning and dyeing lessons, and did custom spinning and knitting. Recently, though, she has sold the herd, put her business on hold, and temporarily relocated in Berkeley, California, while her husband works on his Ph.D. She continues to create wearable art with her spinning and knitting.   © 1992 Kathryn Alexander

Feel like knitting a *tour de force?* You've come to the right spot. Socks like Jean Sherman's elegant, delicate, comfortable pair will not be done tomorrow, but they will be exquisite. You'll feel pampered every time you look at or wear them.

The arrow pattern is adapted from *The Craft of Lace Knitting*, by Barbara G. Walker (New York: Charles Scribner's Sons, 1971), p. 73. The original pattern was contributed to Barbara Walker's book by Hildegard M. Elsner, Aldan, Pennsylvania.

Size: Women's medium.
Yarn: Approximately 1 ounce (23 grams) of *very fine yarn* at about 35 wraps/inch. Jean used a two-ply Merino/silk blend. We found skeins of Paternayan needlepoint yarn to make a test pair from.
Needles: Four double-pointed needles, size 0 (2.25 mm), or size needed to achieve correct gauge.
Gauge: Over lace pattern, 24 sts and 24 rows = 2 inches (5 cm) (**12 sts/inch**).

Cuff and leg. Cast on 72 sts, distribute on 3 needles, and join. Work in k 1, p 1 ribbing for 3 inches (7.5 cm). Change to lace pattern and work for 5½ inches (13.75 cm).

Heel. Adjust sts so that 39 sts (nearly 5 repeats of pattern) are divided and held on 2 needles for top of foot, and remaining 33 sts are on one needle for heel. Working on these 33 sts, proceed as follows. *Row 1:* K 1, purl to last st, k 1. *Row 2:* *K 1, sl 1 knitwise,* repeat * to * across (twisted heel stitch). Repeat these 2 rows until heel flap measures 2 inches (5 cm), ending with a purl row.

Next, turn heel. *Row 1:* K 16, sl 1, k 1, psso, k 1, turn. *Row 2:* P 3, p 2 tog, p 1, turn. *Row 3:* K 4, sl 1, k 1, psso, k 1, turn. *Row 4:* P 5, p 2 tog, p 1, turn. *Row 5:* K 6, sl 1, k 1, psso, k 1, turn. *Row 6:* P 7, p 2 tog, p 1, turn. *Row 7:* K 8, sl 1, k 1,

psso, k 1, turn. *Row 8:* P 9, p 2 tog, p 1, turn. *Row 9:* K 10, sl 1, k 1, psso, k 1, turn. *Row 10:* P 11, p 2 tog, p 1, turn. *Row 11:* K 12, sl 1, k 1, psso, k 1, turn. *Row 12:* P 13, p 2 tog, p 1, turn. *Row 13:* K 14, sl 1, k 1, psso, k 1, turn. *Row 14:* P 15, p 2 tog, p 1, turn. *Row 15:* K 16, sl 1, k 1, psso, k 1 (18 sts remain).

LACE ARROW PATTERN
Repeat of 8 sts and 16 rounds.

Round 1: *Yo, ssk, k 3, k 2 tog, yo, k 1,* repeat * to * around.

Round 2 and all even rounds: Knit.

Round 3: K 1, *yo, ssk, k 1, k 2 tog, yo, k 3,* repeat * to *, ending last repeat with a k 2.

Round 5: *K 2, yo, sl 1, k 2 tog, psso, yo, k 2, p 1,* repeat * to * around.

Rounds 7, 9, 11, 13, and 15: *Ssk, (k 1, yo) twice, k 1, k 2 tog, p 1,* repeat * to * around.

Round 16: Knit.

Instep and foot. Pick up and knit 18 sts along edge of heel; work across 39 sts of instep in lace pattern; pick up and knit 17 sts on other side of heel, and with same needle knit next 9 sts from first needle. Stitches are divided as follows: 27 sts on needle 1, 39 sts on needle 2, 26 sts on needle 3.

Shape instep as follows: On next round, knit to last 3 sts on needle 1, k 2 tog, k 1; on needle 2, work in pattern; at beginning of needle 3, k 1, sl 1, k 1, psso, knit to end of round. Work 1 round even in pattern as established. Repeat these 2 rounds until there are 72 sts again.

Continue working even until foot measures 2 inches (5 cm) less than desired length. Slip 1 st from beginning of needle 2 to end of needle 1 and slip 2 sts from end of needle 2 to beginning of needle 3. Now you have 18 sts on needle 1, 36 sts on needle 2, and 18 sts on needle 3.

Toe. On next round, knit to last 3 sts at end of needle 1, k 2 tog, k 1; on needle 2, k 1, sl 1, k 1, psso, knit to last 3 sts, k 2 tog, k 1; on needle 3, k 1, sl 1, k 1, psso, knit to end of round. Knit 1 round even. Repeat these 2 rounds until 20 sts remain. Divide these sts on 2 needles and graft them together.

Jean Sherman is a master spinner, guest lecturer, workshop leader (including groups at Convergence '86), and an instructor at Olds College, in Olds, Alberta, who uses her skills as a fiber artist to design projects and yarns for use in weaving, embroidery, needlepoint, and crochet, as well as knitting.

←We're putting these socks here to inspire you. You won't want to try them as your first pair, but if you're looking for a rewarding challenge, you've come to the right place. Jean Sherman's Merino/silk socks are elegant and so soft. . . .

Left: Jean Wright's double-knit socks offer a lot of warmth in a lightweight format. You'll get the trick of double knitting pretty quickly if you've already got the basics down.

Right: Ellen Dolson's interpretation of a traditional Turkish sock. Ellen's are knitted from the cuff to the toe (the originals go in the other direction), but have the distinctive heel- and toe-shaping. You can be as wild or as simple as you like with the colors.

Middle: Ansel, who helped with the photo session.

Double-knit socks are not for knitters in a hurry, but the results are very rewarding. Working on the two layers at once does become rhythmic and relaxing after a short while.

Jean Wright's double-knit socks are worked in dark and light yarns, which provide both cushioned warmth and a touch of patterning. The technique she used makes a double-layer cloth that is tightly bonded together throughout the sock. The pattern is her own, inspired by an afghan worked using the same technique.

Jean's white yarn comes from a flock raised on islands off the southwestern coast of Nova Scotia, and the brown wool was a trade for some dog-down spinning. Jean washed and hand carded each fiber, spun the singles from the fold on the double-band, traditional-style wheel her father made for her, and plied loosely to make a soft, medium-weight yarn. The white yarn is approximately worsted-weight, and quite a bit heavier than the dark yarn.

Double-knit Socks

Jean Wright
Stewiacke, Nova Scotia

Size: Women's medium.
Yarn: The main yarn (light) is *worsted-weight*, at 12 wraps per inch and about 1160 yards per pound; the lining yarn is a *sportweight*. Jean used 2½ ounces (70 grams) light (color A) and 2 ounces (56 grams) dark (color B), both in two-ply yarns.

We tested this pattern in 100% wool, Lamb's Pride Superwash from Brown Sheep Company, and used two 100-yard (50-g) skeins each of rose blush and navy heather for a pair of double-knit socks. They worked up just slightly larger than Jean's socks, on the same size needles; because our inner and outer yarns were the same weight, our lining did not fit as smoothly as Jean's. Next time, we'd choose a lighter-weight yarn for the inside.

Needles: Four double-pointed needles in size 3 (3.25 mm), or size needed to achieve correct gauge, and a cable needle or other temporary holder for decreases.
Gauge: In double knit, 19 sts and 24 rows = 4 inches (10 cm) (4¾ sts/inch).

Cuff. With A, cast on 48 sts and distribute on three needles as follows: 15, 15, 18. Join and work in k 2, p 1 rib for 2¾ inches (7 cm). (Jean twists the p stitch, working it through the back loop, to make the rib tighter.)

Leg. Join B. Throughout the sock, knit with both yarns in back and purl with both yarns in front, as noted below under "to double knit."

On first needle: k 1 A and p 1 B in same stitch; in next two sts, k 1 A, p 1 B; then k 1 A and p 1 B in each stitch to

last two sts on needle; k 1 A, p 1 B. Work second and third needles the same way (42 pairs of sts).

Work 1 row plain in double knit, then work 13 rows of chart 1, reversing position of yarns and stitches so that the color patterns appear (white on gray, and gray on white). Continue working plain until sock measures 7½ inches (19 cm).

Heel flap. Work 21 pairs by working one pair, then slipping next pair. Place remaining sts on a needle or holder. Turn work and work all sts back. Twist yarns at beginning of each row to hold fabric together. Continue in this manner until 22 rows have been worked, ending with an all-worked row.

TO DOUBLE KNIT
    With both yarns in back, k A; with both yarns in front, p B (one pair worked).
TO DECREASE
    Slip knit stitch off lefthand needle and onto righthand needle, then slip purl stitch onto cable needle, holding it in back of work. Put knit stitch back on lefthand needle and k 2 tog. Move purl stitch from cable needle back to lefthand needle and p 2 tog.
TO SLIP STITCHES
    With yarns in back, slip knit stitch knitwise; with yarns in front, slip purl stitch purlwise.

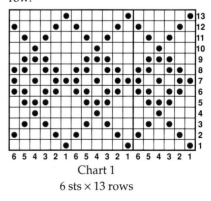

Chart 1
6 sts × 13 rows

Turn heel. *Row 1:* Work 13 pairs, dec 1 pair, work 1 pair, turn.

Row 2: Slip first pair, work 6 pairs, dec 1 pair, work 1 pair, turn.

Row 3: Slip first pair, work 7 pairs, dec 1 pair, work 1 pair, turn.

Row 4: Slip first pair, work 8 pairs, dec 1 pair, work 1 pair, turn.

Row 5: Slip first pair, work 9 pairs, dec 1 pair, work 1 pair, turn.

Row 6: Slip first pair, work 10 pairs, dec 1 pair, work 1 pair, turn.

Row 7: Slip first pair, work 10 pairs, dec 1 pair, work 1 pair, turn.

Row 8: Slip first pair, work 11 pairs, dec 1 pair, turn.

Row 9: Slip first pair, work to end of row (13 pairs on needle).

Instep and foot. On first needle, pick up 12 pairs of stitches from side of heel flap (pick up light sts knitwise from outside, dark sts purlwise from inside). Work the 21 pairs of sts from holder onto second needle. On third needle, pick up 12 pairs from other side of heel flap, then work 7 pairs from heel. Slip remaining heel sts to first needle.

Work plain, decreasing one pair at end of first needle and at beginning of third needle every other rnd until 42 pairs remain. Work even until foot measures 2 inches (5 cm) less than desired length. Work Chart 2 for one round.

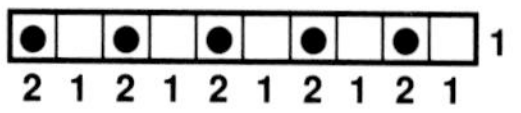

Chart 2
2 sts × 1 row

Toe. Decrease 1 pair at end of first needle, at beginning and end of second needle, and at beginning of third needle every other round until 18 pairs remain. Work first needle. Break yarns, leaving 12-inch (30-cm) tails. Separate the k and p stitches and put the p sts on a holder and tuck inside. Weave light-colored toe stitches together, turn inside out, and weave dark-colored toe stitches. Weave in ends.

Jean writes, "The knitting was completed while I was on my honeymoon in Florida and heading back north. Using ads in Spin·Off as a guide, we enjoyed visiting shops along the route. I am a novice spinner, and it was a treat to talk with others about our shared interest. I have become addicted to the drop spindle I purchased."

Ellen Dolson's Turkish stockings are adapted from a collection of Anatolian designs by Betsy Harrell. Ellen started with a survey of her yarn collection, and chose gray, grape, and rose. She knitted from the top down, instead of in the traditional toe-up direction, and worked the heel last, shaping it like a second toe. Oddly enough, the trickiest part of these stockings is picking up the stitches for the heel. Points to watch carefully are included in the instructions.

Because a double strand of yarn is used for patterning throughout these stockings, they are cushiony and warm. The relatively fine gauge, on the other hand, reduces their bulk to a reasonable weight for use with boots, loose shoes, or Birkenstock sandals.

You could simplify the stocking by using only two colors and by using chart 2 throughout the stocking. Both chart 1 and chart 2 are 35 stitches wide, so they can be interchanged. Chart 1 requires more attention to knit than chart 2.

Ellen suggests that the socks will last longer if a leather sole is added, but considers it a shame to cover up the intricate knitted pattern in the process.

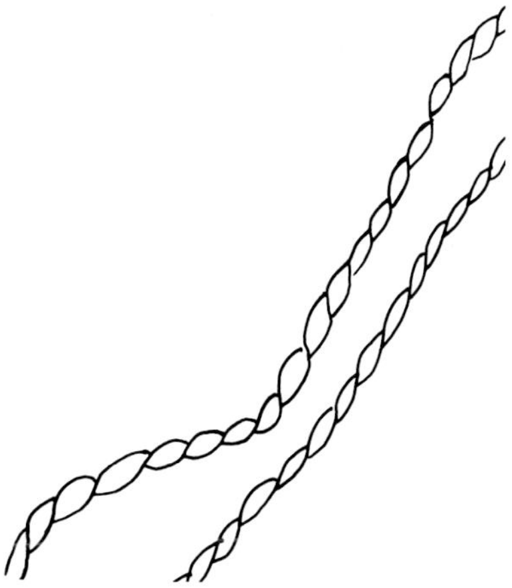

Turkish Stockings

Ellen Dolson
Fortuna, California

Size: Women's medium.

Yarn: 6 ounces (170 grams) of *sport-weight to fingering-weight yarn* at about 13–15 wraps/inch, in colors A (light color), B (dark color), and C (contrasting color). Ellen used a two-ply natural gray Lincoln for the contrasting color, and a 50/50 blend of kid mohair and Southdown, Navajo plied, for the dark and light colors. The dark color was dyed using a commercial dye; the lighter color was obtained by a second dyeing with the same solution, exhausting all of the color. In testing the pattern, we used two different variegated handspun singles, on size 3 (3.25 mm) needles to achieve the correct gauge.

Needles: Four double-pointed needles in size 2 (2.75–3 mm), or size needed to achieve correct gauge.

Gauge: Measured over stockinette stitch in color pattern, **7 sts = 1 inch** (2.5 cm). Check your gauge carefully.

Cuff and leg. Cable cast on 70 sts as follows: *(1 B, 1 A) 17 times, 1 B*. Repeat * to * one more time. Distribute sts evenly on 3 needles and join. Work k 1 B, p 1 A ribbing for 5 rows. Change to stockinette st and begin chart 1 and color sequence: 13 rows A, 13 rows C. Color B is used throughout. Follow chart 1 until leg measures 9 inches (22.5 cm) from beginning.

Heel and foot. With waste yarn, k first 35 sts of next round. (The waste yarn will be taken out later, and these sts will be used to make the heel.) Slip these sts back to lefthand needle, pick up colors A (or C) and B again, and following chart 2, k these same sts for sole (k into waste yarn). Continue chart 1 on last 35 sts of round for instep. Knit in this manner until foot measures 2 inches (5 cm) less than desired length.

Toe. Continuing instep and sole designs, begin decreasing for toe at stitches 4 and 32 of each side every row as follows: *k 1 B, k 1 A, sl 1, k 1 B, psso, k 27, k 2 tog with B, k 1 A, k 1 B,* repeat * to * one more time. Keeping the patterns consistent, decrease 4 sts every round until 18 sts remain. (If you are using Chart 1 on the top of the foot, you will need to keep your wits about you as the patterning area decreases in

Charts 1 and 2 are on the next page

width on every round.) Divide sts on two needles and graft together, using B.

Heel. Pick up 70 sts (35 above waste yarn and 35 below) as you remove the waste yarn. This is a little tricky. We picked up all the stitches across, using one double-pointed needle for the back of the calf and one for the heel section of the sole, before removing the waste yarn. The sts on the back of the calf will be normal. Those on the sole are one-half st "off kilter," and harder to see. When you remove the waste yarn (we picked it out with a crochet hook), some apparent sts will turn out to be yarn-overs of carried pattern yarn. This is okay. Treat them as sts when you work across this area. When knitting the first round, we left the back-of-calf sts on one double-pointed needle, and divided the sole sts on two double-pointed needles, knitting with the fourth. In order to keep the side-seam stitches running uninterrupted, we decreased one st at each side in the first round.

Work heel as for toe. Keep in mind

that you are knitting in the opposite direction, and work the pattern chart(s) from the top down this time.

Finishing. For the tassel at the top of the stocking, we used 8 strands of yarn in all the colors used for knitting. We cut the strands about 8 inches long (20 cm), pulled them through the starting point of the stocking (outside top edge of ribbing) with a crochet hook, braided for 2 inches, tied the braid securely, and trimmed the ends to make a 1-inch (2.5-cm) fringe.

Ellen Dolson worked as an R.N., then retired and went back to school to get a degree in clothing and textiles. She has knitted all her life, and now designs all of her projects.

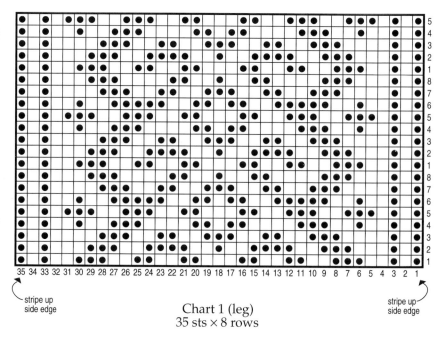

Chart 1 (leg)
35 sts × 8 rows

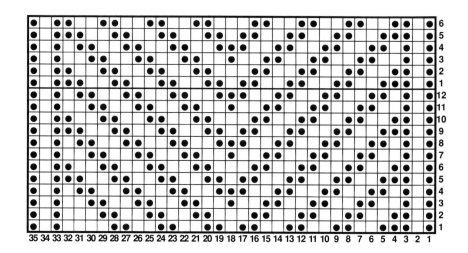

Chart 2 (sole)
35 sts × 12 rows

☐ = color A or C
● = color B

Techniques and abbreviations

cast-on, backward loop

This may have been the first cast-on you ever learned. Worked with one needle, and one ball of yarn. Start with a slip knot on the needle, then make loops on your index finger and slide them onto the needle.

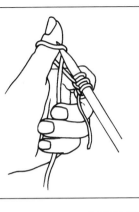

cast-on, cable

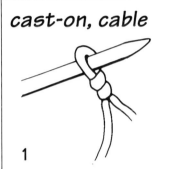

1

Make a slip knot and place it on the left needle.

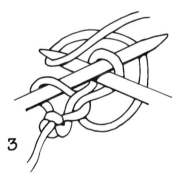

3

Put the tip of the right needle *between* the two sts on the left needle and knit a stitch.

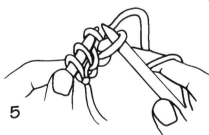

5

Continue, always putting the tip of the right needle between the two most recently formed sts.

Worked with two needles, and one ball of yarn.

2

Insert the tip of the right needle through the loop on the left needle, and knit a stitch. Slip this new stitch from the right needle onto the left needle.

4

Slip the new stitch onto the left needle.

crochet, single

(European: double crochet)

The yarn is carried in back of the work.

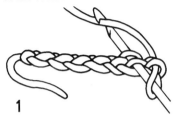

1

Insert hook through base loop, from front to back, and yarn over hook.

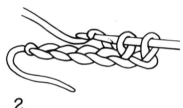

2

Pull through loop, and yarn over hook.

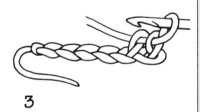

3

Pull new loop through both loops on hook.
   Repeat process on next base loop.

crochet, reverse single

The process is similar to regular single crochet, except that the hook is inserted from back to front through the base loop, and the yarn is carried in front of the work.

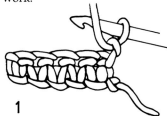

1

Begin by turning at end of row and chaining one.

2

Insert hook through base loop, from back to front, and yarn over hook.

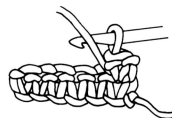

3

Pull through loop, and yarn over hook.

4

Pull new loop through both loops on hook.
    Repeat process on next base loop.

garter st

Worked flat: Knit every row.

Worked in the round: Repeat of 2 rounds. *Round 1:* K around. *Round 2:* P around.

inc   Increase

graft

Grafting is used to join the toe stitches at the end of the sock. Here are general instructions. Each pattern ends with an even number of stitches, divided evenly between two double-pointed needles. Cut the yarn about 18 inches (45 cm) from the sock and thread it into a blunt tapestry needle.

The first two maneuvers are preparation. Holding sock with the two needles next to each other, bring the needle through the first st on the front needle as if to p; pull yarn through, but leave st on needle. Pass yarn around strand at edge of fabric, and put needle through first st on back needle as if to k; pull yarn through but leave st on needle.
    Preparation—Front: purl/leave. Back: knit/leave.
    Now the grafting begins in earnest.
    Put needle through first st on *front* needle as if to k; pull yarn through and remove st from needle.

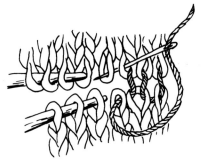

Put needle through second st on front needle as if to p; pull yarn through but leave st on needle.
    Put needle through first st on *back* needle as if to p; pull yarn through and remove st from needle. Put needle through second st on back needle as if to k; pull yarn through but leave st on needle.
    Proceed with this sequence until all sts are woven, with one st remaining:
    Front: knit/remove, purl/leave. Back: purl/remove, knit/leave.
    Pull yarn through last st in established pattern and weave in yarn end before trimming it off.

join

When knitting circularly, the first round of sts must be joined after it is cast on. Cast on the required number of sts and divide them evenly between the double-pointed needles, with one needle free for working.
    Arrange the needles (and sts) in a circle, so that the beginning of the cast-on meets the end. Be sure the sts are not twisted; the "bump" at the bottom of each st needs to be on the bottom of its respective needle.
    It's often wise to place a marker next to the last cast-on st before knitting into the first cast-on st, so you'll know where your rounds start. Knit into the first cast-on st, then proceed as instructed in pattern.

k — Knit.

k 1 b — Knit 1 through back of stitch.

k 2 b — Knit 2 sts through back of stitch separately.

k 2 tog — Knit 2 sts together, as if they were one.

k 2 tog b — Knit 2 sts together through the backs of the sts. Pass right needle tip through both sts, from right to left through backs of loops, put yarn under right needle tip, and draw loop through.

k 2 tog f — Knit 2 sts together through the fronts of the sts (same as k 2 tog). Pass right needle tip through both sts, from left to right through fronts of loops, put yarn under right needle tip, and draw loop through.

psso — Pass the slipped st over.

rnd(s) — Round(s).

seed st

Can be worked on any number of sts. For an even number of sts, worked flat: *Row 1:* * K 1, p 1, * repeat from * to * across. *Row 2:* *P 1, k 1, * repeat from * to * across. For an odd number of sts, worked flat: *Row 1:* K 1, * p 1, k 1, * repeat from * to * across. Repeat this row as required. For an even number of sts, worked in the round: *Round 1:* * K 1, p 1, * repeat from * to * around. *Round 2:* * P 1, k 1, * repeat from * to * around. For an odd number of sts, worked in the round: *Round 1:* K 1, * p 1, k 1, * repeat from * to * around. *Round 2:* P 1, * k 1, p 1, * repeat from * to * around.

sl — Slip.

ssk — Slip two sts separately as if to knit; insert left needle tip from left to right through the fronts of both sts, as if they were one; knit them together.

ssp — Slip two sts separately as if to knit: insert left needle tip from left to right through the backs of both sts, as if they were one; purl them together.

st(s) — stitch(es)

make 1

Increase by lifting.

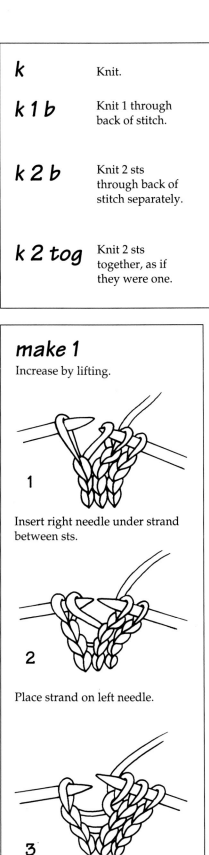

1

Insert right needle under strand between sts.

2

Place strand on left needle.

3

Knit strand as a new st, through back of loop.

p — Purl

pick up knitwise

Work from right to left, with stockinette side facing and yarn in back. Insert needle from front to back, as if to knit, and pull up loop.

pick up purlwise

Work from right to left, with purl side facing and yarn in front. Insert needle from back to front, as if to push, and draw through loop.

stockinette st

Worked flat: Repeat of 2 rows. *Row 1:* K across. *Row 2:* P across. Worked in the round: Knit every round.

Double-knit Socks

Val Slemko
Strathmore, Alberta

Val says that "the idea for these warm double-knit socks came when I was thinking how to help my mother-in-law, who suffers from cold feet. The inner layer is a blend of Merino and French angora. I used Merino top and blended it with the angora on a drum carder. First I picked the two fibers together, then I blended them by putting them through the drum carder twice. On the second time, I separated the original batts into strips and fed them into the carder, moving each strip slowly from side to side to mix the fibers thoroughly.

"I spun the singles Z-twist at 12 twists per inch, and plied S at 6 twists per inch.

"The outer layer is a blend of kid mohair and gray Romney-cross lamb's wool. I spun this blend in the same way, reasoning that the nature of the fiber would make this layer more durable than the inner layer.

"I decided to put a design down the top of the instep to bring some of the inside outside, so the wearer of the socks could not only enjoy the feel of the angora but could also admire it at the same time.

Size: Adult medium.

Yarn: About 4 ounces (110 grams) total of *fingering- to sportweight yarn* at 20 wraps per inch. Val used two-ply yarns, with white Merino/angora for the lining and gray wool/kid mohair for the outside. In testing, we discovered that it's best to use a slightly lighter weight yarn for the lining, which then will lie smoothly in place, as Val's does.

Needles: Four double-pointed needles in size 2 (2.75–3 mm) or 3 (3.25 mm), or size needed to achieve correct gauge.

Gauge: 6 sts = 1 inch (2.5 cm).

Cuff and leg. With 2 strands of the white yarn, cast on 48 sts. (Use double strand of white so the cuffs will be the same thickness as the sock). Divide the sts on 3 needles (16 on each needle) and join. Work in rounds of k 2, p 2 ribbing for 3 inches (7.5 cm).

Join in the gray yarn and drop one strand of white. Knit with gray and purl with white into every stitch, making 16 gray sts and 16 white sts on each needle. Work 4 rounds in double-knit as follows. With both yarns in back, knit with gray. Put both yarns in front and purl with white. Repeat

around. This method knits both layers at the same time. Each *pair* of stitches will be referred to as 1 stitch.

Start pattern, reading the graph from right to left. On the first needle, k 7, work 9 sts from graph, then continue around. Each square on the graph represents one gray knit st for the outer layer and one white purl st for the inner layer. Be sure to follow each knit st with a purl st of the opposite color. Work 6 rounds (one repeat) in pattern, then divide for the heel.

Heel. Put 24 sts, centered on and including the pattern sts, on a holder for the instep. Knit back and forth on the other 24 sts for 2½ inches (6.25 cm) to make the heel flap. Turn the heel by working a series of short rows out

See page 13 for tips on double knitting.

repeat

☐ = white
╱ = gray

from the center as follows. *Note:* When working k 2 tog or p 2 tog, rearrange sts on lefthand needle so you dec 2 grays together or 2 whites tog, not gray and white. *Row 1:* K 14, ssk gray (p 2 tog white), k 1, turn. *Row 2:* K 6, ssk white (p 2 tog gray), k 1, turn. *Row 3:* K 7, ssk gray (p 2 tog white), k 1, turn. *Row 4:* K 8, ssk white (p 2 tog gray), k 1, turn. *Row 5:* K 9, ssk gray (p 2 tog white), k 1, turn. *Row 6:* K 10, ssk white (p 2 tog gray), k 1, turn. *Row 7:* K 11, ssk gray (p 2 tog white), k 1, turn. *Row 8:* K 12, ssk white (p 2 tog gray), k 1, turn. *Row 9:* K 13, ssk gray (p 2 tog white), turn. *Row 10:* K 13, ssk white (p 2 tog gray), turn. *Row 11:* K across.

Instep and foot. Pick up 14 sts on one side of heel flap—knit with gray and purl with white into each loop. Work across the instep sts, following the pattern from the graph. Pick up 14 sts down the other side of the heel flap. Arrange sts as follows: needle 1, half of sts from heel (7 sts), plus 14 sts picked up along one side of heel flap (total of 21 sts on needle 1); needle 2, 24 sts of instep; needle 3, 14 sts picked up along other side of heel flap, plus remaining sts from heel (7 sts) (total of 21 sts on needle 3). Work one complete round.

Left: Ready for more double-knitting? We thought so. Here are Val Slemko's foot-warmers, intended for less rugged use than Jean Wright's socks. The angora lining makes them extra toasty, and extremely soft.

Right: These are socks with work to do. Irene Macrae made them for her sons, who work construction, and now everyone who's heard about them wants some. They work up *very* quickly and wear well.

Shape the instep by working k 2 tog gray (ssp white) 1 st before the instep, and ssk gray (p 2 tog white) 1 st after the instep, on every other round until 48 sts remain (needle 1, 12; needle 2, 24; needle 3, 12). Knit the foot to desired length. End pattern.

Toe. Shape toe by decreasing 4 sts every other round. Work k 2 tog gray (ssp white) at end of first needle. At beginning of second needle, k 2, ssk gray (p 2 tog white). At end of needle 2, k 2 tog gray (p 2 tog white); at beginning of needle 3, ssk gray (p 2 tog white). Repeat these paired decreases until there are 5 sts each remaining on needles 1 and 3, and 10 sts on needle 2. Knit the sts from needle 1 onto needle 3. Slip the white sts to a safety pin and tuck inside the sock while you graft the gray sts together. Turn sock inside out and graft white sts together.

©1992 Val Slemko

Heavy Socks

Irene Macrae
Errington, British Columbia

Here's a simple sock that goes together quickly, has a dash of individuality, uses up small amounts of bulky yarn, and keeps feet from frostbite in serious winter weather. What more could you ask? Our tester actually finished a sock in the "scraps" of time found in two days which included full-time work and parenting. Whee!

Size: Adult medium.

Yarn: 8 ounces (225 grams) of *bulky yarn* at about 10 wraps/inch and small amounts of light and dark yarn for color pattern. Irene used a gray singles for the main color (MC), and small amounts of light and dark yarn for the color work. We tested this pattern in commercial Lopi.

Needles: Four double-pointed needles in size 10 (6–6.5 mm), or size needed to achieve correct gauge.

Gauge: Measured over stockinette stitch, 7 sts = 2 inches (5 cm) (3½ sts/inch).

Cuff and leg. With MC, cast on 32 sts, distribute evenly on 3 needles, and join. Work in twisted rib (k 1 through the back loop, p 1) for 14 rounds or 2½ inches (6.25 cm). Knit 4 rows in MC, then follow the pattern chart. Continue with MC alone. When leg measures 8 inches (20 cm) from beginning, shape calf.

To shape calf, at beginning of next round, k 2, k 2 tog. At end of round, k 2 tog, k 2. Continue on 30 sts without further shaping until sock measures 11 inches (28 cm) or desired length.

Heel. Work the heel flap on 12 sts centered around the calf shaping. Place these sts on one needle by working the first 6 sts of the next round, then sliding the last 6 sts of the previous round to the same needle. (Divide remaining 18 sts on two needles for instep and leave while working heel.) Purl 1 row back on 12 heel sts.

Work heel flap as follows. *Row 1:* With right side facing, *sl 1, k 1,* repeat * to * across. *Row 2:* Purl. Repeat these 2 rows until heel flap measures 2½ inches (6.25 cm), ending with a purl row.

Next, turn heel. *Row 1:* Continuing to work on the 12 sts of the heel, k 6, k 2 tog (leaving 4 sts on lefthand needle), turn. *Row 2:* Sl 1, p 1, p 2 tog (leaving 3 sts on lefthand needle), turn. *Row 3:* Sl 1, k 2, k 2 tog (leaving 2 sts), turn. *Row 4:* Sl 1, p 3, p 2 tog (leaving 1 st), turn. *Row 5:* Sl 1, k remaining sts (8 sts on needle). *Row 6:* Purl. *Row 7:* Knit.

Instep and foot. Pick up 10 sts along left side of heel flap, knit across 18 instep sts, pick up another 10 sts along right side of heel flap. Arrange sts so 18 instep sts are on one needle, and each of the other two needles has 14 sts (4 heel sts plus 10 picked up sts).

To shape instep gusset, k to last 3 sts on needle 1, k 2 tog, k 1. Knit across needle 2. On needle 3, k 1, k 2 tog, k to end of round. Work 1 round even. Repeat these 2 rounds until 32 sts remain. Work straight until foot measures 2½ inches (6.25 cm) less than desired length.

Toe. Arrange sts so there are 16 sts on instep needle and 8 sts on each of the heel needles. On needle 1, knit to last 3 sts, k 2 tog, k 1. On needle 2, k 1, sl 1, k 1, psso, k to last 3 sts, k 2 tog, k 1. On needle 3, k 1, sl 1, k 1, psso, k to end of needle. Work 1 round even. Repeat these 2 rounds until 12 sts remain, ending with needle 1. Slip all heel sts to one needle and graft toe sts.

Irene got into socks for very practical reasons, and somewhat reluctantly. She says, "I am more than a sock person; but I started making these for my sons, who worked on construction. Worn over a pair of cotton socks, there is nothing warmer. Last year, a local electrical contractor ordered a dozen pair to give to his crew at Christmas.

"I raise Angora rabbits and Angora goats, and have two llamas. I especially enjoy planning new yarns and designing sweaters."

X = white
O = dark brown
☐ = gray

22

Hannelore Krieger moved from Germany to Canada thirty years ago. Besides spinning, she especially loves her herb garden. Her fleece-lined socks, like many handspun projects, draw eclectically from a variety of sources.

The idea for fleece-lined garments came from Robin Hansen's *Flying Geese and Partridge Feet*, which showed warm mittens lined with short pieces of hand-rolled fleece. Hannelore thought, "Why not socks?," and figured out a more rugged means of adding the lining. She spun the yarn on her Ashford Traditional wheel, pulled a cast-on technique from *Homespun, Handknit*, and worked with a basic sock shape from an instruction book.

Her first pair looked awkward, because the lined sections were so bulky. On subsequent pairs, she used a three-ply yarn for the leg, and made several changes for the sections that are lined: she switched to a two-ply yarn, worked on smaller needles, and decreased the total number of stitches. Trial and error, the spinning knitter's best allies, triumph again!

Fleece-lined Socks

Hannelore Krieger
Wildwood, Alberta

Size: Men's medium/large.
Materials: *For cuff and leg*, about 3½ ounces (100 g) of dark, *bulky yarn* at about 10–11 wraps/inch and 550–600 yards/pound. Hannelore uses a three-ply, spun from Rambouillet or similar soft wool. *For stripes*, about 1 ounce (28 g) of white wool/angora blend of the same grist as the cuff/leg yarn.

For foot, about 3 ounces (85 grams) of *heavy worsted-weight yarn* at about 12–13 wraps/inch and 650 yards/pound. Hannelore uses a two-ply spun from soft, dark wool. *To reinforce heels and toes*, about 1 ounce (28 g) of yarn of the same grist as the foot yarn. Hannelore uses a dark wool/white mohair yarn.

For lining, about 3½ ounces (100 g) of commercial *pencil roving* or hand-carded wool, pulled out to the thickness of a pencil; the commercial roving which we tested, from Fingerlakes Woolen Mills in Genoa, New York, required three strands held together to achieve this bulk.

Needles: One set each of double-pointed needles in size 5 (3.75–4 mm) and size 3 (3.25 mm), or sizes needed to achieve correct gauge.

Gauge: On smaller needles, worked in the fleece-lining technique with the lighter (foot) yarn and pencil roving, 7 sts = 2 inches (5 cm) (3½ sts/inch). You need to be relaxed and work very loosely to achieve this gauge. Don't pull too tightly!

Cuff and leg. With larger needles and heavier yarn, cast on 48 sts and divide evenly on three needles. The twisted-loop cast on gives a nice, stretchy cuff. Work in k 1, p 1 ribbing to desired length. To make stripes as shown, knit 14 rows brown, 7 white, 7 brown, 6 white, 6 brown, 5 white, and 35 brown.

TECHNIQUE

Note that the entire foot, heel, and toe are lined with roving. The tricky part is learning to carry the roving while you work. When you're knitting around in a circle, it's easy. When you get to back-and-forth work and shaping, it's trickier. We suggest that you make a small trial swatch before starting on the sock.

Loosely cast on 16 sts. Work back and forth in garter st to practice carrying along the roving. Hannelore knits continental style and carries the roving in back, alternately going under and over it as she knits. The roving needs to be knitted in *very loosely*, to make a soft and bulky lining. It should actually puff out on the inside. When the sock is worn, it will become compacted.

Next practice going back and forth in stockinette st, so you'll be able to handle purl rows: you'll need to hold the roving in front, and alternately go over and under it.

Then practice working heel st. On the knit rows, *k 1 under roving, sl 1, k 1 over roving, sl 1*; repeat from * to * across. On the purl rows, purl each st, working under and over the roving.

Now try turning the heel. Watch what's going on, and keep alternating under and over the roving. It doesn't matter if the sock is a little messy on the inside, but be sure you don't pull the roving more tightly as you concentrate on the shaping of the heel!

Okay. Now do a whole sock. . . .

23

Begin foot. Change to smaller needles and work k 2, k 2 tog around. This leaves 12 sts on each needle. Next row, change to lighter yarn and begin knitting-in the pencil-roving lining. Knit 5 rows.

Heel. Knit 16 sts onto one needle for the heel flap and save 20 sts on a holder for the instep. Change from lighter wool to wool/mohair, and k 1, p 7, inc 1, p 7, k 1 (17 sts).

Work heel flap in heel stitch, as follows. *Row 1:* *K 1, sl 1,* repeat from * to * across row, end k 1. Be careful not to pull the yarn too tight behind the slipped sts. *Row 2:* K 1, purl to last st, k 1. Repeat these 2 rows 9 times, ending with a knit row.

Next, turn heel. *Row 1:* K 1, p 8, p 2 tog, p 1, turn. *Row 2:* K 3, sl 1, k 1, psso, k 1, turn. *Row 3:* P 4, p 2 tog, p 1, turn. *Row 4:* K 5, sl 1, k 1, psso, k 1, turn. *Row 5:* P 6, p 2 tog, p 1, turn. *Row 6:* K 7, sl 1, k 1, psso, k 2 (10 sts on needle). Break off wool/mohair yarn and resume using lighter wool yarn.

Instep. On needle 1, pick up 10 sts along left edge of heel flap and knit these onto the needle along with the heel sts. On needle 2, knit across 20 instep sts. On needle 3, pick up 10 sts along right edge of heel flap and knit 5 sts from first needle. (Stitches are divided 15, 20, 15.) *Round 1:* Knit. *Round 2:* On needle 1, k to last 3 sts, k 2 tog, k 1. On needle 2, knit. On needle 3, k 1, sl 1, k 1, psso, knit to end of needle. Repeat these 2 rounds until you have 9 sts on needle 1, 20 sts on needle 2, and 9 sts on needle 3 (38 sts total).

Foot. Continue knitting until foot is 3 inches (7.5 cm) shorter than desired finished length.

Toe. Change to wool/mohair yarn. Knit 3 rounds. *Round 1:* On needle 1, k to last 3 sts, k 2 tog, k 1. On needle 2, k 1, sl 1, k 1, psso, k to last 3 sts, k 2 tog, k 1. On needle 3, k 1, sl 1, k 1, psso, k to end of needle. *Rounds 2 and 3:* Knit.

Repeat these 3 rounds until 19 sts remain. Graft toe sts together.

Hannelore says, "Being no seasoned spinner, I was at first hesitant to participate when the call for socks was an-nounced. But what is there to lose? I love the idea of being able to produce something useful from scratch, especially when it involves working with warm, natural materials in our hectic and artificial mode of life. With "warm" I don't mean only the physical aspect, but the serene feeling that comes from handling a natural product which can be replenished easily with thoughtfulness and good care.

"My spinning is far from perfect, and there's lots of room for improvement. But the yarn can be used. I used to dread these long Alberta winters, but now, with more and more practical hobbies taking over, they could be even longer."

Hansen, Robin, and Janetta Dexter. *Flying Geese and Partridge Feet: Traditional Mittens from Up North and Down East.* Camden, Maine: Down East, 1986.

Ligon, Linda, editor. *Homespun, Handknit.* Loveland, Colorado: Interweave Press, 1987.

Left: The inside of Hannelore Krieger's fleece-lined sock. *Right:* Jean Wright's double-knit sock can be worn with the dark side out (see pages 12 and 13).

← Hannelore Krieger took the idea of fleece-lined mittens and applied it to socks. These have a layer of roving knitted throughout the foot—you can see where the roving is fastened to the main fabric, because it makes a striped pattern on the outside. When worn, the roving felts into a warm cushion.

"Girly Girl" Socks

Robin Fouquette
Cool, California

Robin Fouquette used fiber from her own animals to make the yarn for these socks. She prepared the Rambouillet and angora on a drum carder with fine carding cloth, running it through four times and re-combining the batts on each pass. She spun the yarn with a long draw on her Country Craftsman wheel, and dyed it with Gaywool's "Primula" dye . . . getting a slightly stronger color than she intended.

Her pattern was gathered from a variety of sources, thoroughly blended. The textured pattern was intended for use at the top of a pair of kilt hose featured in *Knitter's* magazine.[1]

Size: Women's medium.

Yarn: 2½ ounces (70 grams) of *sportweight to fingering-weight yarn* at about 16 wraps/inch. Robin used a 70/30 blend of Rambouillet wool and German/French cross angora, spun into a two-ply.

We tested the pattern with Pingouin Corrida 3, a sportweight yarn of about 2000 yards per pound, blended 60/40 from cotton and acrylic.

Needles: Four double-pointed needles each in sizes 0 (2.25 mm) and 2 (2.75–3 mm), or sizes needed to achieve correct gauge.

Gauge: Measured over stockinette stitch on larger needles, 13 sts and 17 rows = 2 inches (5 cm) (6½ sts/inch).

Cuff and leg. Using smaller needles, loosely cast on 56 sts, distribute on 3 needles, and join.

Work k 1, p 1 ribbing for 9 rounds or more, as desired. On last round, dec 2 sts (54 sts). Change to larger needles and work in lace pattern until sock measures 8½ inches (21.5 cm) from beginning.

Heel. Divide the sts for the heel. Starting with the last p st from the previous round, work 27 sts in the lace pattern so that the instep begins and ends with a p st (there will be 3 pattern repeats across the instep, plus the edge p sts). Place these sts on 2 needles or a holder. (If you want, add a sewing thread for reinforcement now, and work it along with the yarn for the heel.) Knit the remaining 27 sts for the

heel flap. Work heel in stockinette st for 2 inches (5 cm), slipping the first st and knitting the last st of each row. End with a knit row.

Turn the heel as follows. *Row 1:* P 16, p 2 tog, p 1, turn. *Row 2:* Sl 1, k 6, k 2 tog b, k 1, turn. *Row 3:* Sl 1, p to 1 st before gap, p 2 tog, p 1, turn. *Row 4:* Sl 1, k to 1 st before gap, k 2 tog b, k 1, turn. Repeat rows 3 and 4 until all sts have been worked. End with a purl row. Break off sewing thread, if you are using it.

Instep and foot. Pick up 1 st every other row along the side of the heel flap. Work across the instep sts in lace pattern (beginning and ending the pattern area with a single p st). Pick up a matching number of sts on the other side of the heel flap. Divide sts so that the instep sts are on 1 needle, and the heel sts are on 2 needles.

To decrease heel gussets, knit across the bottom of the heel and up the side to the last 3 sts before the purl st, k 2 tog, k 1. Work instep pattern, then k 1, k 2 tog b, knit down the side of the gusset. Work 1 round without decreases.

LACE PATTERN STITCH

Repeat of 9 sts and 4 rounds.

Round 1: K 2 tog b, yo, k 3, yo, k 2 tog f, p 2.

Round 2: K 7, p 2.

Round 3: K 2, yo, sl 1, k 2 tog, psso, yo, k 2, p 2.

Round 4: K 7, p 2.

Repeat these 2 rounds until you again have 54 sts. Continue in lace pattern for the instep and stockinette for the sole until sock measures 2 inches (5 cm) less than the length of foot.

Toe. Add reinforcing thread again if desired. Place a marker to divide 27 sts for the top of sock and 27 sts for the bottom. Knit 1 round. On next round, dec 2 sts on the top and 2 sts on the bottom, as follows: k 2, k 2 tog b, k to the last 4 sts of top or bottom, k 2 tog, k 2. Repeat these 2 rounds until 14 sts remain. Graft sts together and sew in ends. *Robin's tip:* Immediately cast on sts for the second sock and work a few rounds.

Robin says, "Our ranch is a family-owned and operated business, involving my parents, my sister and her family, my family, and my brother. We raise purebred Jacob sheep, plus a mixed spinner's flock, Angora rabbits, Angora goats, and a couple of guard llamas. We also have Spinner's Corner, a country store for spinners, knitters, and weavers.

"Some time last year, I became interested in knitting socks. I have been constantly working on sock projects ever since. The interest has spread to our students and customers, who have also expanded into mittens and gloves. These small projects are easy to tuck in a purse and work on when you have a few moments (or are waiting for your child's soccer practice to finish)." © 1992 Robin Fouquette

[1]Bush, Nancy. "Hose." *Knitter's* 5, no. 4 (Issue 13, Winter 1988): pages 16–18.

These lace socks, made of Rambouillet and angora by Robin Fouquette, are soft → and dressy, but quite practical. When she finished them, Robin forged ahead and made matching mittens (mitten pattern not included).

Sweat socks? That's what Claire Ottman calls these, but we think they're much prettier than their name. They *are* sturdy and will take a lot of hard wear, but the texture and the colors make them special enough for any lively souls you love.

Claire Ottman's cabled sweat socks came with a note saying that she has never before offered her work for close scrutiny, but since she had her first spinning lesson in October 1973, she guessed she was "ready to go public."

Claire worked from commercial Romney roving, hand-painted in "Crayola" colors at Ruth's Wheel of Fortune, in New Hampshire. The singles in these socks are her "usual" yarn, spun on a castle-type Haldane wheel and plied on a drop spindle; she says her plying twist is uneven, because as her spindle gets full, she puts in less twist, "because my arm is usually killing me at that point." She persists in drop-spindle plying because she dislikes knitting with lots of joins, and the bobbins on her wheel are too small for her taste.

The idea for the body of these socks came from Bernat's *On Your Toes!* (Handicrafter No. 218, Uxbridge, Massachusetts: Emile Bernat and Sons, 1975). The heel flaps borrow "Eye of partridge stitch" from *Mon Tricot Knitting Dictionary: Stitches and Patterns* (Paris: Mon Tricot, n.d.; page 16), and a garter stitch edge from Elizabeth Zimmermann, *Knitting without Tears* (New York: Charles Scribner's Sons, 1971). Claire says, "I always bend patterns to suit myself."

Cabled Sweat Socks

Claire Ottman
Cherry Valley, New York

Size: Women's medium.

Yarn: 6 ounces (170 grams) of *sportweight to fingering-weight yarn* at about 13 wraps/inch. Claire used hand-painted Romney roving from Ruth's Wheel of Fortune to spin her two-ply yarn. We tested the pattern in a commercially spun, hand-dyed sportweight yarn.

Needles: Two sets of four double-pointed needles in sizes 1 (2.5 mm) and 2 (2.75–3 mm), or sizes needed to achieve correct gauge, one straight needle in the larger size for casting on, and one cable needle. Claire uses two sets of double-pointed needles, because she likes to divide her yarn in half and start both socks at once to maintain even tension and finish both socks at the same time.

Gauge: Measured over stockinette stitch on larger needles, 15 sts and 20 rounds = 2 inches (5 cm) (7½ sts/inch). Measured over cable pattern on larger needles, 20 sts and 20 rounds = 2 inches (5 cm).

Cuff and leg. On larger size straight

CABLE PATTERN

Repeat of 14 sts and 12 rounds.

Rounds 1–4: *K 2, p 2, k 8, p 2,* repeat * to * around.

Round 5: *K 2, p 2, sl next 2 sts to cable needle and hold in *front* of work, k next 2 sts, k 2 sts from cable needle, sl next 2 sts to cable needle and hold in *back* of work, k next 2 sts, k 2 sts from cable needle, p 2,* repeat * to * around.

Rounds 6–10: Repeat round 1.

Round 11: *K 2, p 2, sl next 2 sts to cable needle and hold in *back* of work, k next 2 sts, k 2 sts from cable needle, sl next 2 sts to cable needle and hold in *front* of work, k next 2 sts, k 2 sts from cable needle, p 2,* repeat * to * around.

Round 12: Repeat round 1.

Repeat these 12 rounds.

needle, cast on 72 sts, distribute on three smaller size double-pointed needles, and join. Work k 2, p 2 ribbing for 16 rounds or 1½ inches (3.75 cm), decreasing 2 sts evenly on last round (70 sts).

Change to larger size double-pointed needles and work cable pattern 5 times (60 rounds) or until sock measures 8 inches (20 cm) from beginning. Remember which round you left off on, because you will have to pick up pattern again when you start shaping the heel gusset.

Heel. Starting at the beginning of a round, k 2, slip next 40 sts to a holder or string to be worked later for instep, turn, p 2 sts, then p remaining 28 sts (30 sts on one needle for heel).

Work heel flap as follows. *Row 1 (right side):* Sl 1, k 3, *k 1, sl 1 purlwise with yarn in back,* repeat * to * 11 times, k 3, p 1. *Row 2:* Sl 1, k 3, p 22, k 3, p 1. *Row 3:* Sl 1, k 3, *sl 1 purlwise with yarn in back, k 1,* repeat * to * 11 times, k 3, p 1. *Row 4:* Repeat row 2. Repeat these 4 rows until heel flap measures 2½ inches (6.25 cm), ending with a wrong-side row.

Turn heel as follows. *Row 1:* K 17, ssk, k 1, turn. *Row 2:* Sl 1, p 5, p 2 tog, p

1, turn. *Row 3:* Sl 1, k 6, ssk, k 1, turn. *Row 4:* Sl 1, p 7, p 2 tog, p 1, turn. *Row 5:* Sl 1, k 8, ssk, k 1, turn. *Row 6:* Sl 1, p 9, p 2 tog, p 1, turn. *Row 7:* Sl 1, k 10, ssk, k 1, turn. *Row 8:* Sl 1, p 11, p 2 tog, p 1, turn. *Row 9:* Sl 1, k 12, ssk, k 1, turn. *Row 10:* Sl 1, p 13, p 2 tog, p 1, turn. *Row 11:* Sl 1, k 14, ssk, k 1, turn. *Row 12:* Purl across remaining 18 sts. Break off yarn.

Instep and foot. Join yarn at right edge of beginning of heel flap and with right side facing, pick up 18 sts along side of heel flap. (In order to make the neat, decorative ridge on Claire's original, pick up the stitches at the sides of the heel flap from underneath, so that the outside row of stitches is not covered, and rolls to the outer surface of the sock.) Knit 9 sts of heel onto same needle; onto another needle, k remaining 9 sts of heel and pick up 18 sts along other side of heel flap; sl 40 sts of instep onto a needle and work in pattern across these sts; k 27 sts of first heel needle onto another needle. Work is now joined, and each round will start at center of heel.

To shape gusset, k across needle 1 to last 3 sts, k 2 tog, k 1. Work instep sts in pattern on needle 2. On needle 3, k 1, ssk, k to end. Next rnd, work even in pattern. Repeat these 2 rounds until there are 15 sts on each heel needle (75 sts total). Continue even until foot measures 2 inches (5 cm) less than desired length from center back heel. K the next round, decreasing 10 sts evenly on instep needle.

Toe. *Round 1:* K to last 3 sts of needle 1, k 2 tog, k 1; on needle 2, k 1, ssk, k to last 3 sts, k 2 tog, k 1; on needle 3, k 1, ssk, k to end of needle. *Round 2:* K all sts. Repeat these 2 rounds until there are 5 sts on each heel needle (20 sts total), ending with needle 1. Put all sole sts onto one needle. Break off yarn, leaving a 12-inch (30-cm) tail. Weave sole and instep sts together. Weave in ends. Steam lightly.

Claire Ottman demonstrates spinning and weaving at the Farmer's Museum and is active in the Leatherstocking Spinners Guild, along with fellow sock contributor Garry Aney.

Spiral Rib Socks

Garry Aney
Mohawk, New York

Size: Adult medium.
Yarn: 6 ounces (170 grams) of *worsted-weight yarn* at about 12½ wraps/inch. Garry spun two-ply yarns from Corriedale hand-raised wool and Coopworth roving from Louët.
Needles: Four double-pointed needles in size 2 (2.75–3 mm) or 3 (3.25 mm), or size needed to achieve correct gauge.
Gauge: Measured over spiral ribbing, 6½–7 sts = 1 inch (2.5 cm).

Cuff and leg. Cast on 66 sts, distribute evenly on 3 needles, and join. Place a marker at the joining spot. Work in k 3, p 3 ribbing for about 6¾ inches (17 cm) or desired length.

Ankle and foot. Begin spiral ribbing by moving the ribs over 1 st; that is, begin next round with p 1, k 3, and then continue in k 3, p 3 ribbing.

This is a great project for new sock knitters (there's no heel to turn) or for those who need to make something that is satisfying but doesn't require constant attention.

Garry's spiral rib socks began with a pattern in an issue of *Spin·Off*. His intricate and interesting yarns add variety and fun to the mix.

The wool for one ply is Corriedale and crosses, drum carded from acid-dyed layers of ten different colors, following Deb Menz's techniques for making multicolored batts. Garry worked on a base of blues, adding warm, cool, and neutral contrasts. For the second ply, Garry painted Coopworth roving with Lanaset dyes, using another of Deb's techniques.

The bulk of the sock is made of a two-ply incorporating both yarns, although the toes are worked with the Coopworth plied on itself. To keep the socks balanced—and make sure he didn't run out of yarn at an awkward point—Garry divided his stock of the Corriedale/Coopworth yarn in half and worked both socks simultaneously, on two sets of needles.

Work 3 more rounds following the stitch sequence you just established. Continue in this manner, always moving over one more st every fourth round, using the marker as a guide for where to change, until sock is 15¾ inches (39 cm) long, or 1 inch (2.5 cm) less than desired length.

Toe. Knit one round even. On next round, k 1, k 2 tog around. Repeat these 2 rounds until there are 8 sts remaining. Break off yarn, leaving about 8 inches (20 cm). Thread blunt needle and run through remaining sts two times; fasten off. Weave in ends.

Garry D. Aney works on his family's dairy farm, and also demonstrates spinning and weaving at the Farmer's Museum in Cooperstown, New York. He is very active in the Leatherstocking Spinning Guild (fellow guild member Claire Ottman's work is also featured here).

Top: In doubt about making socks? Start here! Garry Aney used a classic, heelless, spiral rib design for the basic structure. He worked it in a cheerfully nubby and brightly colored yarn, but you can use what you've got that's about worsted weight. The ribbing stretches to fit.
Bottom: Jude Daurelle's apparently quiet socks have a lot of muscle to them. The soles are entirely reinforced with nylon thread. They won't wear out for quite a while. The delicate coloration of her yarn belies their sturdiness; surprise! (Instructions start on page 39.)

This hound's-tooth sock has toes that point right or left, depending on which foot it's meant for. Marty Rather designed them in worsted-weight handspun *(near right and left above)*. These socks are quite heavy—they would go well in Birkenstocks or, if you can stand to cover them up, in boots, or they can be slippers.

Our testers worked the pattern in two different yarns, to demonstrate how much flexibility there is in choosing yarns for socks. Each yarn was worked to the specified gauge of 5½ stitches/inch; Marty's handspun corresponds approximately to a commercial yarn that would work up at about 5 stitches/inch. She worked more densely than this, for durability.

All the socks were knitted on the same number of stitches, and they all fit! We did try our socks on as we worked—it's fun, and saves lots of trouble.

Right: This is a sportweight commercial yarn, one that would normally knit up at about 6 stitches/inch. It's the lightest of the three socks, and will fit inside a shoe.

Center: This is a heavy worsted-weight yarn, one that would normally knit up at about 4½ stitches/inch. It's a dense fabric, very slipper-like, and would keep toes toasty around a drafty house.

These socks have highly opinionated toes, each with a different point of view. My feet do not come to a point in the middle of the foot, nor do they taper down to a wedge on the sides. They are shaped more like a rectangle —with a bottom, two sides, and a top—that tapers at an angle to the right or left at the toes. To emphasize that difference (in a rather subtle way) I have carefully knitted a right sock (white on gray) and a left sock (gray on white). The two socks look nearly identical but can be distinguished by different-colored ribbing and by toes that slant in different directions.

To give my socks a rectangular shape (after turning the heel), I decrease along the instep until there are fewer stitches across the bottom of the foot (sole) than there are for the two sides and across the top. I knitted the sole in a different pattern to emphasize this shape. In this case, I used a diamond pattern.

These thick and warm socks fit loosely and make ideal slippers. If you want a snugger fit, use smaller needles and a tighter gauge. The yarn used in these socks was some of the first yarn I spun, so it is rather thick and uneven and accounts for the heavy nature of the socks.

Hound's-tooth Socks

Marty Rather
Brentwood, Tennessee

Size: Women's small/medium (see yarn notes).

Yarn: *Worsted-weight yarn,* at about 11 wraps per inch. Marty spun her yarn from white Romney and gray Coopworth. The blue and gray socks were knitted from Emu Superwash, a DK or sportweight yarn; this resulted in a lighter weight sock. Because this pair needed to fit a women's extra-large foot, we worked 12 more rows in the foot (continuing the diamonds) before shaping the toe. The purple and black socks were knitted from Brown Sheep Company's Lamb's Pride yarn, a heavy worsted-weight yarn, at 5 sts/inch, for a more slipper-like effect.

Needles: Four double-pointed needles each in sizes 3 (3.25 mm) and 5 (3.75–4 mm), or sizes needed to achieve correct gauge.

Gauge: 5½ sts/inch (2.5 cm) and 6 rows/inch on larger needles.

Cuff and leg. Cast on 52 sts on smaller needles. Join and work k 1, p 1 ribbing for 7 rows. Change to larger needles, stockinette st, and hound's-tooth pattern for 6–7 inches (15–18 cm).

Heel. Divide the sts so that there are 25 sts for the heel on one needle and 27 sts for the top and sides of the foot divided between two needles. Work back and forth on the 25 heel sts in hound's-tooth pattern, always slipping the first st of each row, for 2–2½ inches (5–6.25 cm), ending with a purl row.

The heel is turned in the next 10 rows. The first two rows are worked in the main color and the diamond pattern begins on the third row (see chart on next page). *Row 1:* K 15, ssk, k 1, turn. *Row 2:* Sl 1, p 6, p 2 tog, p 1, turn. *Row 3:* (Begin diamond pattern.) Sl 1, k 7, ssk, k 1, turn. *Row 4:* Sl 1, p 8, p 2 tog, p 1, turn. *Row 5:* Sl 1, k 9, ssk, k 1, turn. *Row 6:* Sl 1, p 10, p 2 tog, p 1, turn. *Row 7:* Sl 1, k 11, ssk, k 1, turn. *Row 8:* Sl 1, p 12, p 2 tog, p 1, turn. *Row 9:* Sl 1, k 13, ssk, turn. *Row 10:* Sl 1, p 13, p 2 tog.

Hound's-tooth pattern
4 sts × 4 rows

Instep. Work across the remaining 15 heel sts in the established pattern. Pick up 7 sts along the left side of the heel flap (pick up in diamond pattern, according to chart, and pick up the 7th st through the body of the sock to avoid a hole at the join). Work across the 27 top-and-sides-of-the-foot sts in hound's-tooth pattern. Pick up 7 sts along the right side of the heel flap (pick up in diamond pattern, according to chart, and pick up the first st through the body of the sock). There will be a total of 29 sts for the sole (instep plus bottom-of-the-foot sts).

Work the hound's-tooth pattern for the top and sides of the foot and the diamond pattern for the instep and bottom of the foot. Decrease 1 st on each side of the instep (4 sts total) every other row until 21 sts remain on the sole (48 sts total).

Foot. Continue working the 27 sts for the top and sides of the foot in hound's-tooth pattern and the 21 sts for the sole in diamond pattern, following the chart, until the foot reaches halfway up your little toe, or to the desired length for toe shaping.

Toe. The bottom of the toe is

33

worked in the diamond pattern as shown on the chart, and the top is worked in stripes as follows: *k 1 main color, k 1 contrast color*, repeat from * to * across. The toe decreases are worked on either side of st number 1 and st number 21 of the sole sts (ssk worked to the right of these sts and k 2 tog worked to the left of these sts; 2 sts decreased at each side).

Before you begin, choose a big toe side and a little toe side. To make the toe of the sock angle like the toes on your foot, the decreases are worked at a faster rate on the little toe side than on the big toe side. On the first row, decrease 2 sts on the little toe side and 2 sts on the big toe side. Then decrease 2 sts on the little toe side every other row 3 times and then every row 5 times. *At the same time*, decrease 2 sts on the big toe side every 4th row once, then every 3rd row once, and then every other row twice.

To make sure this sequence of decreases is right for your gauge and your foot, try on the sock every few rows to check the shaping against your foot and adjust the frequency of decreases if necessary. Use more frequent decreases for a sharper angle, and less frequent decreases for a gentler angle.

When the decreases are completed, 7 sts remain on the sole of the foot and 14 sts remain on the top. To make the same number of sts on both sides, k 2 tog across the 14 top sts using the main color. Graft together the remaining sts.

Marty writes, "My Swedish grand-mother taught me to knit mittens when I was ten and she was in her late seventies. Grandma Martha (for whom I am named) came to the United States in her twenties, was met by her fiancee, Swan Peterson, and rode a horse to North Dakota, where they lived in a sod house and raised four children. By the time I came along, in the next generation, she still refused to speak English. The time when she showed me how to knit was one of the few times we really tried to communicate with each other.

"Twelve years ago, when I discovered Elizabeth Zimmermann's books, I began to knit in earnest. I loved the idea of making my own patterns, inventing my own rules, and later reinventing them again. I just love the enthusiasm in the books and videos produced by Elizabeth and her daughter, Meg Swansen. But, of course, I have to change all their patterns to suit me.

"I started spinning in May 1991, when I acquired a used Ashford spinning wheel. I had just met a group of spinners and got caught up in their enthusiasm. We have such fun together, and they have taught me a lot about spinning and raising sheep."
© 1992 Marty Rather

Left foot diamond pattern;
reverse toe shaping for right foot

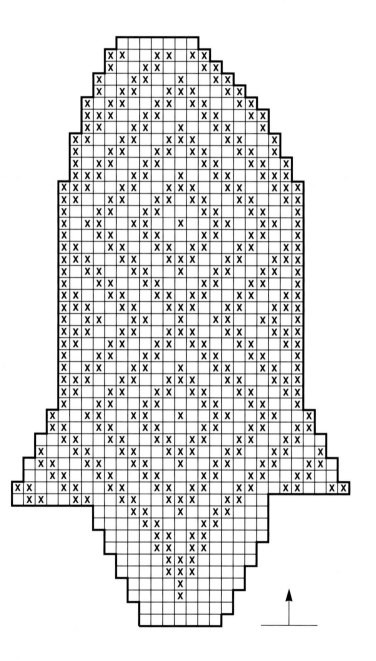

When Margaret Jaeger began knitting socks in earnest around twenty years ago, she began with the charting formula in Chapter 14 of Ida Riley Duncan's *The Complete Book of Progressive Knitting* (New York and London: Liveright, 1968). Having worked with the idea for so many years, she's no longer sure which parts are original and which are her own modifications. Two pairs of her socks appear in this publication, on this page and page 38.

Both Fair Isle charts for these knee socks were adapted from Sarah Don, and the little heel decoration on the boot socks came from Elizabeth Zimmermann. The patterns actually used up odds and ends. The Fair Isle heel pattern is intended to be visible when the socks are worn with clogs or sandals, but the resulting double thickness of yarn also provides heel reinforcement if the socks are worn with closed shoes.

Fair Isle Knee Socks for Clogs or Sandals

Margaret Jaeger
Kensington, California

Size: Women's medium.

Yarn: In *sportweight yarn*, approximately 5½–6 ounces (155–170 grams) of main color (MC) and small amounts of light, medium, and dark pattern yarns. Original yarn is two-ply handspun at 13½ wraps per inch. The gray was spun from roving, breed(s) unknown; contrasting colors were from dyed roving. We tested the pattern in 4 Pingouins, a machine-washable wool yarn from Pingouin, in DK or sportweight.

Needles: Four double-pointed needles in sizes 2 (2.75–3 mm) and 3 (3.25 mm), or sizes needed to achieve correct gauge.

Gauge: 27 sts = 4 inches (10 cm) on larger needles (6¾ sts/inch).

Cuff and leg. With larger needles and MC, cast on 80 sts. Change to smaller needles, divide evenly on 3 needles, join, mark beginning of round for center back, and work 12 rounds in k 2, p 2 ribbing (about 1¼ inch, or 3 cm).

Change to larger needles and work 12 rounds of stockinette st (approx. 1¼ inches, or 3 cm). Following chart, work 19 rows of calf pattern. Rejoin MC and work 1 round.

Begin the calf to ankle shaping. Decrease on next round as follows. At beginning of needle 1, k 1, k 2 tog, k to end. At end of third needle, k to last 2

sts, then sl 1, k 1, psso. (There will be 1 st between these paired decreases; it is the first st on needle 1 and is the center back st.) Repeat decrease round every sixth round 13 times until 54 sts remain.

Work even until stocking measures 15 inches (37.5 cm) or desired length from knee to ankle.

Heel. Divide sts for heel as follows. On first needle, 27 sts (with center back st centered and subsequent 13 sts of next round worked so yarn is at left of needle 1); on second needle, 13 sts; on

third needle, 14 sts. Work back and forth in stockinette st for 20 rows on the 27 sts of needle 1, beginning with a purl row and slipping first st of each row. Work Fair Isle heel pattern from chart on rows 2 through 14.

Next, turn heel. *Row 1:* Sl 1, p 15, p 2 tog, p 1, turn. *Row 2:* Sl 1, k 6, sl 1, k 1, psso, k 1, turn. *Row 3:* Sl 1, p 7, p 2 tog, p 1, turn. *Row 4:* Sl 1, k 8, sl 1, k 1, psso, k 1, turn. *Row 5:* Sl 1, p 9, p 2 tog, p 1, turn. *Row 6:* Sl 1, k 10, sl 1, k 1, psso, k 1, turn. *Row 7:* Sl 1, p 11, p 2 tog, p 1, turn. *Row 8:* Sl 1, k 12, sl 1, k 1, psso, k

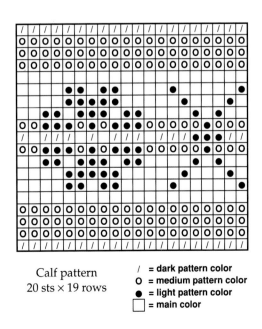

Calf pattern
20 sts × 19 rows

/ = dark pattern color
O = medium pattern color
● = light pattern color
□ = main color

These socks were great fun to make. They're fine enough to fit a variety of purposes, but they work up quickly. Both pairs are by Margaret Jaeger. *Left:* These hiking boot socks have a little garter-stitch detail along the edge of the heel. *Right:* Keep going, add some color patterning, and you get these Fair Isle knee socks: classic and playful, at once.

1, turn. *Row 9:* Sl 1, p 13, p 2 tog, p 1, turn. *Row 10:* Sl 1, k 14, sl 1, k 1, psso, k 1 (17 sts remain).

Instep and foot. Pick up 12 sts along right selvedge of heel flap. (Pick up approximately 1 st per slipped edge st, fudging where necessary. You should be able to find at least one extra st at top of instep; picking up this one will prevent a possible gap at the beginning of the gusset decrease.) Knit across sts from needles 2 and 3. Pick up another 12 sts along left selvedge of heel flap, for a total of 68 sts. Divide sts as follows, with center back st now falling as first st of needle 1: On needle 1, 21 sts (center back st, plus 8 heel sts, plus 12 picked up); on needle 2 for instep, 27 sts; on needle 3, 20 sts (12 picked up plus 8 heel sts).

Next work decreases for instep gussets. Knit 1 round even. On next round, knit to last 3 sts of needle 1, k 2 tog, k 1; knit across needle 2; on needle 3, k 1, sl 1, k 1, psso, k to end of round. Repeat these 2 rounds 7 times, decreasing to a total of 54 sts, divided 14, 27, 13.

Work foot straight until 2 inches (5 cm) less than desired length, measured from base of heel flap (about 7½ inches, or 19 cm, for women's shoe sizes 6 to 7; 8–8½ inches, or 20–21.5 cm, for shoe sizes 8 to 9).

Toe. *Round 1:* On needle 1, k to last 3 sts, k 2 tog, k 1. On needle 2, k 1, sl 1, k 1, psso, k to last 3 sts, k 2 tog, k 1. On needle 3, k 1, sl 1, k 1, psso, k to end. *Round 2:* Knit around. Repeat these 2 rounds until 18 sts remain. Graft sts together.

© *1992 Margaret Jaeger*

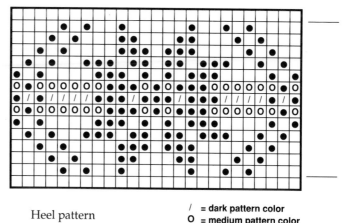

Heel pattern
25 sts × 13 rows

/ = dark pattern color
O = medium pattern color
● = light pattern color
☐ = main color

Hiking Boot Socks

Margaret Jaeger
Kensington, California

These are the socks to knit for everyday, and everywhere. They are simple and straightforward, but worked at a gauge which produces a supple, not-too-bulky fabric. Commit this pattern to memory, and treat everyone around you to happy feet. . . .

Size: Women's medium.
Yarn: 3½ ounces (100 grams) of *sportweight yarn* at about 12½ wraps per inch. Margaret used up odds and ends of three-ply handspun, made from white and brown New Zealand Romney blended on a drum carder.
Needles: Four double-pointed needles, size 3 (3.25 mm), or size needed to achieve correct gauge.
Gauge: 27 sts = 4 inches (10 cm) (**6¾ sts/inch**).

Cuff and leg. Cast on 56 sts, divide on 3 needles, join, mark beginning of round for center back, and work in k 2, p 2 ribbing for 3½ inches (8.75 cm).

Change to stockinette st and continue to work around for another 4 inches (10 cm). (The proportion of ribbing to stockinette st is a matter of personal preference and may be altered.)

Heel. Divide sts for heel as follows. On needle 1, 28 sts (with center back marker centered, and subsequent 14 sts of next round worked so yarn is at left end of needle 1). On needles 2 and 3, 14 sts each for instep (total 28 sts). Work back and forth on 28 sts of needle 1 for 20 rows as follows: *Row 1 (wrong side):* Sl 1, k 3, p 20, k 3, p 1. *Row 2:* Sl 1, k 27. Alternate rows 1 and 2 to make a bit of garter st pattern that adds interest to heel.

Next, turn heel. *Row 1:* Sl 1, p 15, p 2 tog, p 1, turn. *Row 2:* Sl 1, k 6, sl 1, k 1, psso, k 1, turn. *Row 3:* Sl 1, p 7, p 2 tog,

p 1, turn. *Row 4:* Sl 1, k 8, sl 1, k 1, psso, k 1, turn. *Row 5:* Sl 1, p 9, p 2 tog, p 1, turn. *Row 6:* Sl 1, k 10, sl 1, k 1, psso, k 1, turn. *Row 7:* Sl 1, p 11, p 2 tog, p 1, turn. *Row 8:* Sl 1, k 12, sl 1, k 1, psso, k 1, turn. *Row 9:* Sl 1, p 13, p 2 tog, p 1, turn. *Row 10:* Sl 1, k 14, sl 1, k 1, psso, k 1 (18 sts remain).

Instep and foot. Pick up 12 sts along right selvedge of heel flap. (Pick up approximately 1 st per slipped edge st, fudging where necessary. You should be able to find at least one extra st at top of instep; picking up this one will prevent a possible gap at the beginning of the gusset decrease.) Knit across sts from needles 2 and 3 onto one needle for instep. Pick up another 12 sts along left selvedge of heel flap for a total of 70 sts. Divide sts as follows, removing marker, as center back will now fall between needles 1 and 3: on needle 1, 21 sts (9 heel sts plus 12 picked up); on needle 2 for instep, 28 sts; on needle 3, 21 sts (12 picked up plus 9 heel sts).

Decrease for instep gusset. Repeat the following 2 rounds 7 times, decreasing to a total of 56 sts, divided 14, 28, 14: *Round 1:* Knit even. *Round 2:* Knit to last 3 sts of needle 1, k 2 tog, k 1; knit across needle 2; on needle 3, k 1, sl 1, k 1, psso, k to end of round.

Work foot straight until 2 inches (5 cm) less than desired length, measured from base of heel flap (about 7½ inches, or 19 cm, for women's shoe sizes 6 to 7; 8–8½ inches, or 20–21.5

cm, for shoe sizes 8 to 9).

Toe. *Round 1:* On needle 1, k to last 3 sts, k 2 tog, k 1. On needle 2, k 1, sl 1, k 1, psso, k to last 3 sts, k 2 tog, k 1. On needle 3, k 1, sl 1, k 1, psso, k to end. *Round 2:* Knit even around. Repeat these 2 rounds until 16 sts remain. Graft together the toe sts.

Margaret writes, "My mother insisted I learn to knit my own socks after I took up backpacking in Girl Scouts and soon went through the handknit argyles I found preserved in the back of my father's dresser drawer. However, I really got serious about socks when I learned to spin, developed a serious fiber addiction, and acquired a mountain-climbing husband, all about the same time.

"The husband is an international wildlife biologist, and I have spun and knitted my way through Ethiopia, Kenya, and Bangladesh. We have exercised our socks from the Great Rift Valley of Africa to the Himalayas of India and Nepal. We now live in Berkeley, California, where there are fewer mountains to climb, but the socks are great with sandals in the winter time.

"I also knit sweaters, hats, scarves, gloves, mittens, ear bands, shawls, and so forth. But socks remain my favorite form of expression; I sort of specialize in them, and these specimens are only a portion of our current supply-in-residence. Sometimes I even sell them."

© 1992 Margaret Jaeger

These beautiful socks are intended for use outdoors, with cotton liners, and *durability* is emphasized throughout their spinning and structure.

Jude selects a wool that is strong but not too scratchy. She prefers to work with a medium Romney, a Corriedale, or a Lincoln hogget, spinning a sturdy three-ply yarn with a substantial amount of twist. Then she knits a ribbed cuff and leg, for secure fit. When she gets to the foot, she maintains the ribbing down its top, while working the sole in stockinette with a strand of nylon reinforcing yarn throughout.

Practical as they are in concept and execution, these particular socks are also beautifully colored. Jude took her inspiration from muted Amish color harmonies and rainbow-dyed the finished yarn with Cushing dyes, in mauve, wine, navy, green, and turquoise.

Fundamental Socks

Jude Daurelle
Midvale, Utah
(shown on page 31)

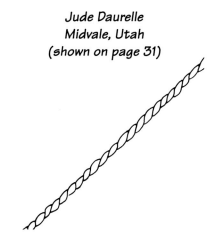

Size: Women's medium.

Yarn: 6 ounces (170 grams) of *worsted-weight yarn* at about 10 wraps/inch and 600 yards/pound, with a twist angle of about 25°. Jude spun three-ply yarns; her singles measured about 25 wraps/inch. In addition, Jude uses 1 ounce of heel-and-toe yarn as an integral part of the sock, worked throughout the sole of the foot.

Needles: Five double-pointed needles in size 4 (3.5 mm) or 5 (3.75–4 mm), or size needed to achieve correct gauge. Jude uses needles about two sizes larger for her cast-on, then switches to her gauge-appropriate needles.

Gauge: In stockinette, **5 sts = 1 inch** (2.5 cm).

Cuff and leg. Using larger needles, cast on 40 sts; divide on 3 needles so

sts are distributed 12, 18, and 10. Join, change to smaller needles, and work in k 2, p 2 ribbing for 6 inches (15 cm), or until cuff is as long as you like.

Heel. On needle 1, k 12 sts. Attach nylon heel-and-toe yarn and k heel flap as follows on the 18 sts of needle 2: *Row 1:* Sl 1, * k 1, sl 1, * repeat from * to * across row, end k 1. *Row 2:* Sl 1, purl across remaining 17 sts. Alternate these two rows until heel flap measures 2 inches (5 cm).

Next, turn heel. *Row 1:* K across 18 sts of heel. *Row 2:* Sl 1, p 9, p 2 tog, p 1, turn. *Row 3:* Sl 1, k 4, k 2 tog, k 1, turn. *Row 4:* Sl 1, p 5, p 2 tog, p 1, turn. *Row 5:* Sl 1, k 6, k 2 tog, k 1, turn. *Row 6:* Sl 1, p 7, p 2 tog, p 1, turn. *Row 7:* Sl 1, k 8, k 2 tog, k 1, turn. *Row 8:* Sl 1, p 9, p 2 tog, turn. *Row 9:* Sl 1, k across (11 sts remain).

Instep and foot. Position sock so heel flap faces you and cuff portion is on the bottom. Using both threads, pick up 12 sts along left edge of heel flap. (Pick up approximately 1 st per slipped edge st, fudging where necessary.) Place these sts on the heel flap needle.

Combine the sts from the next two needles; you will have 22 sts, beginning and ending with 2 purls. Drop the nylon thread. Using only the main yarn, work p 2, k 2 ribbing across these 22 sts, keeping them on needle 2. This ribbing portion continues from the cuff to the toe decreases.

Carry the nylon thread loosely across the top (or inside) of each sock. Using both yarns, pick up another 12 sts along right edge of heel flap. K 4 sts from heel, then k 2 tog onto this needle (needle 3, with 17 sts). There are a total of 56 sts: on needle 1, 17 sts; on needle 2 for instep, 22 sts; on needle 3, 17 sts. Place a small safety pin in the first st of needle 1 at the middle bottom of the foot, to mark the beginning of the rounds.

Decrease for instep gusset. *Round 1:* K across needle 1 with both yarns, carry nylon yarn loosely across top and with main yarn rib 22 on needle 2, k across needle 3 with both yarns. *Round 2:* With both yarns, k to last 3 sts of needle 1, k 2 tog, k 1. Drop nylon thread, carrying it loosely inside the sock, and rib across needle 2. With

←The sock in progress *(left)* shows strands of reinforcing thread. When complete, the strands are trimmed away and their ends disappear *(right)*.

both yarns, begin needle 3 with k 1, ssk, then k to end of round. Repeat these 2 rounds 7 times, until 10 sts each remain on needles 1 and 3 (42 sts total).

Work foot straight until 2 inches (5 cm) less than desired length, measured from base of heel flap (about 7 1/2 inches, or 19 cm, for women's shoe sizes 6 to 7; 8–8 1/2 inches, or 20–21.5 cm, for shoe sizes 8 to 9; for most of our testers, keep going . . .).

Toe. *Round 1:* On needle 1, k to last 3 sts, k 2 tog, k 1. On needle 2, k 1, ssk, k to last 3 sts, k 2 tog, k 1. On needle 3, k 1, ssk, k to end. *Round 2:* Knit even around. Repeat these 2 rounds until 16 sts remain. K the sts of needle 1 onto the end of needle 3. Graft together the toe sts. Trim off the excess nylon yarn (carried across foot); the ends will remain securely fastened in the knitted fabric of the sole.

Jude Daurelle, when not making long-lasting socks, has been concentrating on weaving handspun linen and cotton with, as she says, "happy results." She spins "almost any fiber" on her Schacht wheel, knits and crochets in addition to weaving, and has a family that pitches in.

Overview of socks by yarn size and gauge

Designer	Sock	Type of yarn*	Size of yarn (wraps/inch)	Gauge (sts/inch)	Page
Jean Sherman	Lacy	0	35	12	11
Mary Spanos	Christmas	0 – 3	approx. 18	many	53
Kathryn Alexander	Entrelac	1 – 2	15 – 18	8 – 8$\frac{1}{3}$	7
Ruth Blazenko	Very basic	2 – 3	16	6$\frac{1}{2}$	51
Wilma Dibelka	Blue-and-white	2 – 3	16	6	48
Ellen Dolson	Turkish	2 – 3	13 – 15	6$\frac{1}{2}$ – 7	15
Barbara Evans	Three-color	2 – 3	18	6 – 6$\frac{2}{3}$	42
Robin Fouquette	Girly girl	2 – 3	16	6$\frac{1}{2}$	26
Claire Ottman	Cabled	2 – 3	13	7$\frac{1}{2}$	29
Val Slemko	Double-knit	2 – 3	20	6	20
Margaret Jaeger	Hiking boot	3	12$\frac{1}{2}$	6$\frac{3}{4}$	38
Margaret Jaeger	Fair Isle knee	3	13$\frac{1}{2}$	6$\frac{3}{4}$	35
Garry Aney	Spiral rib	3 – 4	12$\frac{1}{2}$	6$\frac{1}{2}$ – 7	30
Jean Wright	Double-knit	3 – 4	12 – 14	3$\frac{3}{4}$	13
Jude Daurelle	Fundamental	4	10	5	39
Marty Rather	Hound's-tooth	4	11	5$\frac{1}{2}$	33
Susan Atkins	Felted hot sox	4 – 5	11	4	44
Joan Gooth-Buchanan	Fireside	5	9	3$\frac{1}{4}$	47
Hannelore Krieger	Fleece-lined	5	10 – 13	3$\frac{1}{2}$ (lined)	23
Irene Macrae	Heavy	5	10	3$\frac{1}{2}$	22

Overview of socks by designer

Designer	Sock	Type of yarn*	Size of yarn (wraps/inch)	Gauge (sts/inch)	Page
Kathryn Alexander	Entrelac	1 – 2	15 – 18	8 – 8$\frac{1}{3}$	7
Garry Aney	Spiral rib	3 – 4	12$\frac{1}{2}$	6$\frac{1}{2}$ – 7	30
Susan Atkins	Felted hot sox	4 – 5	11	4	44
Ruth Blazenko	Very basic	2 – 3	16	6$\frac{1}{2}$	51
Jude Daurelle	Fundamental	4	10	5	39
Wilma Dibelka	Blue-and-white	2 – 3	16	6	48
Ellen Dolson	Turkish	2 – 3	13 – 15	6$\frac{1}{2}$ – 7	15
Barbara Evans	Three-color	2 – 3	18	6 – 6$\frac{2}{3}$	42
Robin Fouquette	Girly girl	2 – 3	16	6$\frac{1}{2}$	26
Joan Gooth-Buchanan	Fireside	5	9	3$\frac{1}{4}$	47
Margaret Jaeger	Hiking boot	3	12$\frac{1}{2}$	6$\frac{3}{4}$	38
Margaret Jaeger	Fair Isle knee	3	13$\frac{1}{2}$	6$\frac{3}{4}$	35
Hannelore Krieger	Fleece-lined	5	10 – 13	3$\frac{1}{2}$ (lined)	23
Irene Macrae	Heavy	5	10	3$\frac{1}{2}$	22
Claire Ottman	Cabled	2 – 3	13	7$\frac{1}{2}$	29
Marty Rather	Hound's-tooth	4	11	5$\frac{1}{2}$	33
Jean Sherman	Lacy	0	35	12	11
Val Slemko	Double-knit	2 – 3	20	6	20
Mary Spanos	Christmas	0 – 3	approx. 18	many	53
Jean Wright	Double-knit	3 – 4	12 – 14	3$\frac{3}{4}$	13

*Key for type of yarn

0 = very fine   1 = laceweight   2 = fingering   3 = sportweight   4 = worsted-weight   5 = bulky

Three-color Knee Socks

Barbara Evans
Corona, California

Although these socks are knitted in stockinette through the leg area, the alternation (and twisting together) of the colors produces an intriguing corrugated texture. The foot is worked in a modified rib stitch, incorporating color changes and texture. The results look complicated, but once you've got the sequences in your head, they move right along!

Size: Women's medium.

Yarn: *Sportweight to fingering-weight yarn,* at about 18 wraps/inch. Approximately 200 yards of main color (MC; light blue) and 150 yards each of contrasting colors B (dark blue) and C (red). Barbara spun the light blue from Merino top. The contrasting colors were both spun from Hott Soxx batts, an 80/20 blend of wool and nylon from Custom Colors. All three yarns were spun fairly fine with lots of twist and then Navajo plied. Barbara washed all skeins in hot, sudsy water and rinsed in hot water. Then she "shocked" the yarn by plunging the hot skeins into cold water before hanging them to dry with no added weight.

We tested these socks with 4 Pingouins, a machine-washable commercial wool yarn from Pingouin in DK or sportweight; it is lighter than some sportweight yarns. We used three 1¾-ounce (50 g) balls of the main color and one each of the accents— however, we used one accent in larger amounts on one sock, and the reverse for the other sock.

Needles: Five double-pointed needles, size 4 (3.5 mm) or size needed to achieve correct gauge, and one size D crochet hook. See testing note under gauge.

Gauge: In color pattern, 20 sts = 3 inches (7.5 cm) (6⅔ sts/inch). *Testing note:* Our yarn was less elastic than the original, and the tester's legs are 13 inches (33 cm) at the calf. To achieve a good fit, we worked at 18 sts = 3 inches (7.5 cm) (6 sts/inch) on size 5 (3.75–4 mm) needles. We worked our ribbing on size 3 (3.25 mm) needles, and worked on a larger number of stitches, as indicated in brackets.

Cuff and leg. With MC, cast on 60 sts loosely on larger needles, divide among 4 needles, and join without twisting. With smaller needles, work in k 1, p 1 rib for 20 rounds or 2½ inches (6.25 cm). [On last row of ribbing, increase 8 sts evenly around.] Mark center back stitch (CBS) and begin color pattern, knitting all following rounds.

Work chart 1 from bottom to top, working 9 repeats of the block pattern, changing colors as necessary one stitch *before* the CBS. [For longer legs, work more repeats of block pattern. We worked 12.] Note that each block is simply 3 sts of one color, 1 st of second color; twist the yarn of the second color behind the center st of the 3 sts of the first color *every* row. This produces a slight "rib" in the center of each block, and also avoids floats on the inside which would catch toes!

On blocks 5 and 6 [and 7] decrease 1 st each side of CBS after rows 2 and 6 of the block (maintain the pattern); 8 [12] sts decreased, 52 [56] sts remain.

Heel. After 9 [12] blocks, divide for heel as follows: 12 sts, CBS, and next 12 sts on one needle (25 sts for heel), 13 [15] sts on one needle and 14 [16] sts on another needle (27 [31] sts for top of foot).

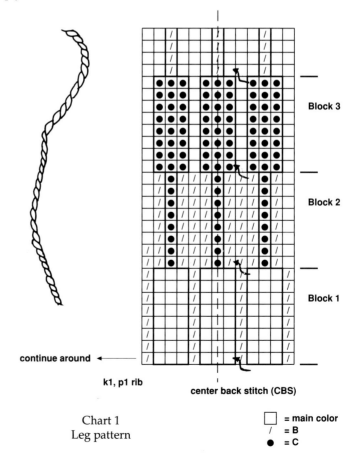

continue around ◄—

k1, p1 rib

center back stitch (CBS)

Block 3

Block 2

Block 1

Chart 1
Leg pattern

☐ = main color
/ = B
● = C

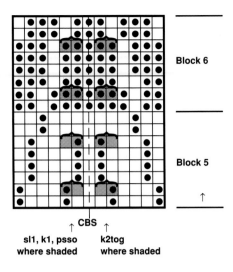

Chart 2
Calf decreases

sl1, k1, psso
where shaded

k2tog
where shaded

↑ CBS ↑

---

working on 54 sts, there will be one wider rib section at the bottom of the foot; simply maintain existing pattern.]

Toe. Divide sts for toes as follows: CBS (bottom of foot) and next 12 sts on one needle, next 13 sts on second needle, next 13 [14] sts on third needle, last 13 [14] sts on fourth needle.

Begin toe shaping. Using only B or C, k 1 round. Knit across to last 3 sts of needle 1 (right side of foot), k 2 tog, k 1. On needle 2, k 1, sl 1, k 1, psso, knit across top of foot to last 3 sts of needle 3 (top left side), k 2 tog, k 1. On needle 4, k 1, sl 1, k 1, psso, k to end of needle. Repeat this decrease *every* round until 10 sts remain. Graft together 5 sts of top of foot and 5 sts of bottom of foot.

Finishing. With B, work 1 round of single crochet around top of cuff. Then work 1 round of reverse single crochet in C. Fasten off.

Barbara says, "I've been spinning for fifteen years, and knitting and crocheting for over thirty years. Ironically, I didn't start knitting socks when I lived in Ohio. It took a move to southern California and meeting a wonderful German spinner and knitter named Ingrid Penrose to inspire me.

"My first pair of socks was made for my husband, Frank. I tucked them into his duffle bag when he went trout fishing in the High Sierras. Sure enough, he fell into the icy creek; and when he found those socks in his bag, he made a trip into town to call me and thank me for 'saving his life'—making my efforts more than worthwhile!

"If it's fiber, I'll happily spin it. My favorite projects are whatever I'm working on at the moment, and whatever I'm planning to do next."

© 1992 Barbara Evans

Using color B or C, work heel stitch as follows across the 25 heel sts. *Row 1:* *K 1, sl 1*, repeat from * to * across, end k 1. *Row 2:* Purl. Alternate these two rows until piece is square (2–2½ inches, or 5–6.25 cm), ending with a knit row.

Next, turn heel. *Row 1:* P 13, p 2 tog, p 1, turn. *Row 2:* Sl 1, k 2, sl 1, k 1, psso, k 1, turn. *Row 3:* Sl 1, p 3, p 2 tog, p 1, turn. *Row 4:* Sl 1, k 4, sl 1, k 1, psso, k 1, turn. *Row 5:* Sl 1, p 5, p 2 tog, p 1, turn. *Row 6:* Sl 1, k 6, sl 1, k 1, psso, k 1, turn. *Row 7:* Sl 1, p 7, p 2 tog, p 1, turn. *Row 8:* Sl 1, k 8, sl 1, k 1, psso, k 1, turn. *Row 9:* Sl 1, p 9, p 2 tog, p 1, turn. *Row 10:* Sl 1, k 10, sl 1, k 1, psso, k 1, turn. *Row 11:* Sl 1, p 11, p 2 tog, turn. *Row 12:* Sl 1, k 11, sl 1, k 1, psso (13 sts remain).

Instep and foot. Now, alternating MC and B, pick up 13 sts along side of heel on needle 1. Continuing with the color alternation, knit across top of foot sts on needles 2 and 3, dividing sts evenly between them. Then pick up 13 sts along other side of heel flap on needle 4. Work instep and foot in modified rib st as shown in chart 3; work 1 round to establish pattern.

Keeping to modified rib st, work gussets (k 2 tog at end of needle 1; sl 1, k 1, psso at beginning of needle 4) *every* round until 52 [54] sts remain. Work even until foot measures 1¼ inches (3 cm) less than desired length. [If

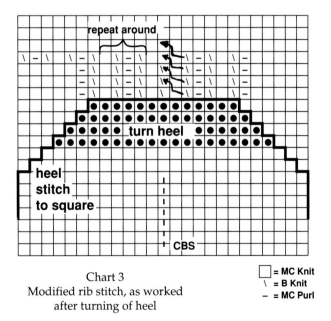

repeat around

turn heel

heel
stitch
to square

CBS

Chart 3
Modified rib stitch, as worked after turning of heel

☐ = MC Knit
\ = B Knit
– = MC Purl

Hot Sox

Susan Atkins
Reynoldsburg, Ohio

Susan Atkins calls these "hot sox," because they are so toasty. They were the first project made on her *own* spinning wheel: a Christmas present, after six months of playing with a borrowed wheel. She needed a project that would give her immediate gratification, could be used frequently, and would be easy to care for.

Size: Women's large, but size can be adjusted in the felting process.

Yarn: 4 ounces (110 grams) loosely spun, loosely plied *bulky or heavy worsted-weight* wool yarn at about 11 wraps/inch. The success of the felting process depends upon the variety of wool you choose; make a test swatch and process it (as described below) to estimate your results. If using a commercial substitute, avoid superwash wools, which have been chemically treated to prevent felting.

Needles: Four double-pointed needles in size 8 (5–5.5 mm), or size needed to achieve correct gauge.

Gauge: 4 sts = 1 inch (2.5 cm) unfelted.

Cuff and leg. Cast on 40 sts and distribute on 3 needles (10, 10, 20). Use your most elastic cast-on, if you have mastered a variety. Work in k 1, p 1 ribbing for 2 inches (5 cm). Knit 1 round in stockinette stitch.

Heel. On needle holding 20 sts, continue to work in stockinette st for 20 rows, slipping first st of each row. Then turn heel, as follows. *Row 1:* Purl 10 sts, p 2 tog, p 1, turn. *Row 2:* Sl 1, k 1, k 2 tog, k 1, turn. *Row 3:* Sl 1, p 2, p 2 tog, p 1, turn. *Row 4:* Sl 1, k 3, k 2 tog, k 1, turn. *Row 5:* Sl 1, p 4, p 2 tog, p 1, turn. *Row 6:* Sl 1, k 5, k 2 tog, k 1, turn. *Row 7:* Sl 1, p 6, p 2 tog, p 1, turn. *Row 8:* Sl 1, k 7, k 2 tog, k 1, turn. *Row 9:* Sl 1, p 8, p 2 tog, turn. *Row 10:* Sl 1, k 8, k 2 tog (10 sts remain). Don't fret about how your decreases lean; they get lost in the felting process.

Instep and foot. On needle with heel sts (needle 1), pick up and knit 10 sts along edge of heel flap. On needle 2, k the instep sts (10 + 10). On needle 3, pick up and knit 10 more sts along other side of heel flap and then k 5 sts from first needle. The sts are now distributed 15, 20, 15. Knit 1 round plain.

To shape gusset, on next round, k 2 tog at end of needle 1, knit even across instep, ssk at beginning of needle 3. Knit 1 round plain. Repeat these 2 rounds until 40 sts remain (10, 20, 10). Knit even until foot is as long as your foot (you need the extra length for felting).

Toe. On next round, k 2 tog, k 1 at end of needle 1; at beginning of needle 2, k 1, ssk, work to last 3 sts of same needle, k 2 tog, k 1; at beginning of needle 3, ssk. Knit 1 round even. Repeat these 2 rounds until 8 sts remain, ending with needle 1. Divide sts onto 2 needles and graft together.

Finishing. Toss socks in the washer with a regular load of laundry and then put them through the dryer. Repeat this process until you get the size you want. Susan finds that about three times gives maximum shrinkage. If you shrink the socks fully, you can care for them like regular socks. If the size is satisfactory after fewer washings, you can machine wash, but skip the dryer. You will find that this finish is very forgiving and will hide a lot of spinning and knitting flaws.

Susan writes, "I have been a weaver for about seven years. I took to spinning because I wanted to follow the process of fabric construction from start to finish. I own a Lendrum wheel, and have learned to spin by osmosis. My local guild (Central Ohio Weavers Guild) has monthly spin-ins, and is very active in offering demos at local art shows. It was at one of these demos that I started to spin.

"I started to teach myself to knit when I was ten. In addition, I make various kinds of lace: tatted, bobbin lace, and knitted lace.

"I live with my husband, John, and two cats, named Molly and Aja. My goals are to weave every twill, spin a yarn fine enough for lace, knit a shawl, tat a large doily, create a bobbin-lace fan; I secretly dream of being a stand-up comedienne. Many of my friends say that the last of these tasks is the only one I am close to accomplishing."

Left: These are "hot sox," by Susan Atkins—the product of pure wool yarn, quickly knitted, and flung into the washer and dryer. Abandon your inhibitions and make some today!

Right: In a more sedate mood, take on Barbara Evans' three-color knee socks. The color patterning comes from a simple rotation of yarns. There are two strands throughout, so the socks are cushiony and warm.

45

These socks are very quick to make. Joan knits them from singles, plied yarns, and various fibers, in any combination that will give her 9 wraps per inch. When using separate balls of fiber, she knits from them that way, without plying them together first. Her sample socks show a number of ways to use up odds and ends of yarn.

Fireside Socks

Joan Gooth-Buchanan
Manlius, New York

Size: Adult medium.

Yarn: About 150–200 yards of yarn at 9 wraps per inch (this corresponds to a *bulky* weight); yardage depends primarily on length of cuff.

Needles: One straight needle, size 11 (7–7.5 mm); one pair *or* four double-pointed needles, size 8 (5–5.5 mm); four double-pointed needles, size 10½ (6.5–7 mm), or size needed to achieve correct gauge.

Gauge: 13 sts = 4 inches (10 cm) (**3¼ sts/inch**).

Cuff and leg. *Loosely* cast on 28 sts, using the size 11 needle, and work onto size 8 needles in k 1, p 1 or k 2, p 2 rib (your choice). Divide evenly on 3 needles, join (being careful not to twist sts), and rib for 2–2½ inches (5–6.25 cm).

Change to size 10½ needles for leg. Continue in rib or change to stockinette st and work to desired length (about 7 inches, or 18 cm). Joan prefers a stockinette leg, but works both ways.

Heel. Divide sts for heel as follows. *Needle 1:* K 7; slide preceding 7 sts from needle 3 to start of needle 1 (14 sts) *Needles 2 and 3:* Divide remaining sts evenly between these needles, and reserve for instep.

Work heel flap on sts of needle 1 in stockinette, slipping first st of each row. Heel flap measures between 2 and 2¼ inches (5–5.7 cm); end with a purl row.

Next, turn heel. *Row 1:* Sl 1, k 7, k 2 tog, k 1, turn. *Row 2:* Sl 1, p 3, p 2 tog, p 1, turn. *Row 3:* Sl 1, k 4, k 2 tog, k 1, turn. *Row 4:* Sl 1, p 5, p 2 tog, p 1, turn. *Row 5:* Sl 1, k 6, k 2 tog, turn. *Row 6:* Sl 1, p 6, p 2 tog, turn. *Row 7:* Sl 1, k across (8 sts on needle).

Instep and foot. Pick up 7–8 sts along right selvedge of heel flap. Knit across 14 sts on instep needle, continuing in pattern of your choice across instep. Pick up another 7–8 sts along left selvedge of heel flap. Divide sts as follows. On first needle, 11–12 sts (picked up sts plus 4 of heel sts; on second needle for instep, 14 sts; on third needle, 11–12 sts (picked up sts plus 4 of heel sts).

Decrease for instep gusset: Repeat the following 2 rnds until there are 7 sts on each of the heel needles (there will be 14 sts on the instep needle). *Round 1:* Knit even. *Round 2:* Knit to last 3 sts of first needle, sl 1, k 1, psso, k 1; knit across instep; on third needle, k1, k 2 tog, k to end of round.

Work foot straight until 2 inches (5 cm) less than desired length, measured from base of heel flap (about 7½ inches or 19 cm for shoe sizes 6 to 7; 8 to 8½ inches or 20–21.5 cm for shoe sizes 8 to 9).

Toe. *Round 1:* On needle 1, k to last 3 sts, sl 1, k 1, psso, k 1. On needle 2, k 1, k 2 tog, k to last 3 sts, sl 1, k 1, psso, k1. On needle 3, k 1, k 2 tog, k to end of needle. *Round 2:* Knit. Repeat these 2 rounds until 12 sts remain. Place sts from needles 1 and 3 together on one needle, so there are two needles with 6 sts on them, and finish the row so that the yarn is on the right side of the needle in back. Graft together the toe sts.

Joan Gooth-Buchanan has been a knitting enthusiast since she was fourteen, but found it difficult to find others of like mind. Her sister and some of her friends were spinners and had great times together; Joan decided to learn to spin so she could join their gatherings and find knitting buddies. She used to raise Angora rabbits on her Gateway Farm, so she would have fiber to work with. Now the only resident four-legged animal is her dog, but she has barrels of angora fiber and yarns in her studio for her future projects. She says she's an old-fashioned practical person whose projects have to be functional; as a result, she knits a lot of socks. (She also admits to making crazy hats.) She likes entering the competitions at county and state fairs and has won a number of red ribbons and honorable mentions, but her goal is a blue.

← Your leftover yarns are about to assume a starring role. Joan Gooth-Buchanan winds together a number of yarns so their combined weight equals a single bulky strand. Then—starting on a mere 28 stitches—she whips out cheerful, useful socks: no two pairs the same!

Blue-and-white Socks

Wilma Dibelka
Mount Shasta, California

Wilma Dibelka is a nurse; her husband is a farmer. They live on Mount Shasta and get snowed in during the winter, so that's when Wilma does a lot of spinning and knitting. These socks were knitted from a pattern which Wilma has carried around in her head for ages. She doesn't recall where the original came from, but says it has to have dated from about 1947 or 1948. She likes it because it "really is quite simple, and makes a nice pair of socks." The pair in the photo has purl stripes every inch or so.

Size: Adult medium.

Yarn: 3½ ounces (100 grams) of *sportweight to fingering-weight yarn* at about 16 wraps/inch. Wilma used three-ply yarn.

Needles: Four double-pointed needles each in size 3 (3.25), or size needed to achieve correct gauge, and in size 5 (3.75–4 mm) for casting on. If you would like a snugger cuff, you will also need four double-pointed needles in size 2 (2.75–3 mm), or one size smaller than the needles used for the body of the sock.

Gauge: 6 sts = 1 inch (2.5 cm) on size 3, or size used for body of sock.

Cuff and leg. With largest needles, cast on 44 or 48 sts, depending on how you like your cuff: snug or loose. Change to smaller needles (size 3 on 44 sts, or size 2 on 48 sts) and work in k 2, p 2 ribbing for 2 inches (5 cm).

If you have 44 sts, increase 4 sts (48 sts total). If you have 48 sts, do not increase. Change to size 3 needles, if you are not already on them. Work pattern (knit 10 rounds, purl 2 rounds) until sock measures 9½ inches (23.75 cm), or desired length of cuff and leg.

Heel. Divide sts in half and place 24 sts at top of foot on a holder. On 24 sts at back of sock, work heel stitch as follows: *Row 1:* Knit across. *Row 2:* *Sl 1, p 1,* repeat * to * across. Repeat these 2 rows 17 times total (34 rows), ending with a purl row.

Next, turn heel. *Row 1:* Sl 1, k 12, sl 1, k 1, psso, k 1, turn. *Row 2:* Sl 1, p 3, p 2 tog, p 1, turn. *Row 3:* Sl 1, k 4, sl 1, k 1, psso, k 1, turn. *Row 4:* Sl 1, p 5, p 2 tog, p 1, turn. *Row 5:* Sl 1, k 6, sl 1, k 1, psso, k 1, turn. *Row 6:* Sl 1, p 7, p 2 tog, p 1, turn. *Row 7:* Sl 1, k 8, sl 1, k 1, psso, k 1, turn. *Row 8:* Sl 1, p 9, p2 tog, p 1, turn. *Row 9:* Sl 1, k 10, sl 1, k 1, psso, k 1, turn. *Row 10:* Sl 1, p 11, p 2 tog, p 1 (14 sts remain). Knit 1 row.

Instep and foot. On needle 1, pick up 17 or 18 sts along side of heel flap. On needle 2, knit across 24 sts of instep. On needle 3, pick up 17 or 18 sts along other side of heel flap and knit next 7 heel sts from needle 1. Knit the remaining 7 heel sts onto the working needle, then continue knitting with the sts on needle 1 (adding them to that group). Decrease 1 st at end of needle 1 (k 2 tog, k 2) and at beginning of needle 3 (k 2, sl 1, k 1, psso) *every other round* until 48 sts remain. Knit even until foot measures 2 inches (5 cm) less than desired length.

Toe. Next round, on needle 1, k to last 3 sts, k 2 tog, k 1; on needle 2, k 1, sl 1, k 1, psso, k to last 3 sts, k 2 tog, k 1; on needle 3, k 1, sl 1, k 1, psso, knit to end. Knit 1 round even.

Repeat these 2 rounds until 12 to 20 sts remain, depending on shape of foot (for pointed toes, decrease to 12 sts). Work sts on needle 1, then place sts on 2 needles and graft together.

Wilma writes, "I am a long-standing knitter of socks, having done my first pair when I was 17. I started with a pair of argyles, the supreme overconfidence of youth, made as a gift for my father. Bless his soul, he wore them.

"By the time I started dating my future husband, three years later, I was pretty good at socks. To help win his heart, I made socks for him. I guess he assumed they were part of the package, and I've been making socks ever since. That's about 42 years now.

"I started spinning about five years ago. Last year I set about learning to spin fine.

"These are just everyday socks; nothing fancy. They began with a bag of mill ends, sent to me by a friend. I pulled them into roving, without sorting colors. I spin on an Ashford Traveler with a high-speed flyer. I am not a technical spinner. I spun about 9 ounces as fine as felt right, then made a three-ply which was about a sportweight yarn. I was pleasantly surprised when the yarn turned out to look like denim. My husband is a farmer and wears a lot of denim."

Wilma Dibelka has knitted more socks than she can remember. This is one of her favorite patterns, embellished with random purl stripes along the leg. You can put in the purl stripes, or leave them out, or make any little textured decoration that you invent. →

What to do with a fine, singles yarn of French angora, with an undetermined amount of yardage? Ruth Blazenko thought this would be perfect for making a pair of socks to wear around the house when she felt the need to be pampered. She made a three-ply yarn of angora, silk, and flick-carded lamb's wool, then dyed the result in Kool-Aid . . . and was plenty surprised when the silk quickly absorbed the dye, leaving very little for the other fibers. She used three packages of Tropical Punch for the three ounces of yarn.

Ruth likes using a smaller needle on a twisted ribbing, which increases the elasticity of the cuff. Her ribbing needles are generally two sizes smaller than her primary needles.

Very Basic Socks

Ruth Blazenko
Calgary, Alberta

Size: Women's medium.

Yarn: 3½ ounces (100 grams) of *sportweight to fingering-weight yarn* at about 16 wraps/inch. Ruth used a three-ply, composed of one ply of cultivated silk, one ply of Romney lamb's wool, and one ply of French angora. She dyed the yarn with three packages of Tropical Punch Kool-Aid. The silk absorbed most of the Kool-Aid in 15 minutes; the wool and angora absorbed very little.

Needles: Four double-pointed needles in sizes 1 (2.5 mm) and 2 (2.75–3 mm), or sizes needed to achieve correct gauge.

Gauge: 6½ sts = 1 inch (2.5 cm).

Cuff and leg. With larger needles, cast on 60 sts, distribute on 3 needles, and join. Work 1 round in k 2 (twist each st), p 2 ribbing, then change to smaller needles and continue in rib for 2¾ inches (7 cm).

Change to larger needles, and knit 3 inches (7.5 cm) in stockinette st.

Heel. Divide sts in half. 30 sts will be used for instep, the other 30 sts for heel. Work heel flap as follows: *Row 1 (right-side row):* *Sl 1 knitwise, k 1,* repeat * to * across. This will give a

twisted-stitch heel pattern. *Row 2:* Sl first st, then p across. Repeat these 2 rows for 2–2½ inches (5–6.25 cm), ending with a right-side row.

Next, turn heel. *Row 1:* P to center of row (15 sts), p 1, p 2 tog, p 1, turn. *Row 2:* Sl 1, k 3, sl 1, k 1, psso, k 1, turn. *Row 3:* Sl 1, p to one st before turning, p 2 tog, p 1, turn. *Row 4:* Sl 1, k to one st before turning, sl 1, k 1, psso, k 1, turn. Repeat Rows 3 and 4 until all sts are used (16 sts remain), ending with a right-side row. The final two rows will be: *Row Y:* Sl 1, p 14, p 2 tog, turn. *Row Z:* Sl 1, k 14, sl 1, k 1, psso.

Instep and foot. With right side still facing, pick up 1 st in each st along left edge of heel flap on needle 1. On needle 2, work instep sts. On needle 3, pick up same number of sts along right edge of heel flap as on left edge; then k half of heel sts (8 sts). As you work 1 round even, start needle 1 with the remaining 8 sts of the heel and the picked-up sts on the left edge of the heel flap.

Begin gusset shaping. On next round, work to last 3 sts on needle 1, k 2 tog, k 1. Knit even across instep sts. At beginning of needle 3, k 1, ssk. Knit 1 round even. Repeat these 2 rounds

until you have 60 sts, the same amount as for leg, then try sock on. You may want to decrease further as Ruth did on this sock (52 sts).

Knit even in stockinette st until sock measures to first joint of big toe (about 2 inches, or 5 cm, less than desired length).

Toe. When shaping the toe, make sure there are an equal number of sts on top and bottom of foot (the top is on needle 2; the bottom is on needles 1 and 3). When you reach 3 sts before the end of needle 1 (right edge of foot), k 2 tog, k 1. On needle 2, k 1, ssk, knit to 3 sts before the end, k 2 tog, k 1. On needle 3, k 1, ssk, knit to end. Knit next round plain. Repeat these 2 rounds until you have 20 to 24 sts left; work sts on first needle. Divide sts onto 2 needles and graft together.

Ruth says, "I have been spinning for the past three years, after starting out with a pair of French Angora rabbits. At present, I breed and show Giant Angoras. I am also going into the third level of the Master Spinners' program up here. I was taught to knit by my grandmother when I was seven. I have been knitting for thirty-two years . . . it seems like forever!"

← "Very basic" is what Ruth Blazenko calls her socks—and they are, if your idea of basic is this wonderful. The fiber is angora and wool, dyed with Kool-Aid, and the shaping is simply perfect.

These tiny stockings pack a lot of intriguing texture into a tiny space. Mary suggests using them for Christmas ornaments; young daughters in the testers' vicinity wanted pairs, for their most special dolls. In either case, they are an appropriate project for using fine, luxury-quality sample skeins of yarn. The finished size of your sock, or socks, will depend on the yarn and needles you choose, and there is lots of room for variety.

The only hard part of this project is keeping the needles in the stitches. There aren't many stitches and fine metal needles are slippery. Knitting tightly helps. Using a larger size needle for a cable needle, rather than the typically used smaller needle, helps keep the needle in its stitch while you maneuver.

Christmas Stocking Ornament

Mary Spanos
Alabaster, Alabama

Size: Approximately 3½" (8.75 cm) long.

Yarn: The wool for this stocking was combed on 4-pitch English combs and spun on a Schacht wheel. The singles were spun at 31 wraps per inch, and two-plied at 4 twists per inch. A smooth, rather than fuzzy, yarn shows the pattern more distinctly. The twist in this yarn was set by passing the skein over the steam from a boiling tea kettle.

We tested the pattern with two-ply Harrisville Shetland, a yarn between fingering and sportweight.

Needles: Five double-pointed German lace needles, size 00; cable needle, preferably slightly larger than the basic needles.

Gauge: Varies, depending on materials.

Cuff and leg. Cast 32 sts onto 1 needle using the backward loop method. Don't make a slip knot for the first loop; just start making backward loops. Having no slip knot on the first st makes the hem look neater. Knit the first row, being vary careful not to pull the cast-on yarn, then divide the sts among 4 needles. Join, and work 4

more rnds, knitting in the rnd. Work the next rnd as follows: * yo, k 2 tog, repeat from *. This is a little difficult to do with tightly knitted sts, but it's soon done. Knit 5 rnds.

The hem is made by folding the knitting at the yarn-over rnd, picking up the cast-on sts (or rather the cast-on loops) one at a time, and knitting them with the sts on the needles. Be careful that each st and loop that are knitted together are from the same column of sts.

The design of 9 sts is repeated 4 times around. Rnd 1 includes increases that will result in the required 36 sts. These increases are only done in the first rnd, and then those new sts are purled. Cables cause the fabric to draw in, so increases are necessary to make the stocking body the same size as the hem. When it's time to go back to plain knitting for the heel and toe, the increased sts will be decreased.

Work rnds 1 through 5 once, and then repeat rnds 2 through 5 until there are five twists in the pattern cable, ending with rnd 3.

Rnd 1: * K 1 b, p 1, k 1 b, p 1, make 1, k 1 b, p 1, k 1 b, p 1, repeat from * around.

Rnd 2: * K 1 b, p 1, cable 2 front (place knit st on holder, hold in front, purl next st, knit through back of held st), cable 2 back (place purl st on holder, hold in back, knit through back of knit st, purl the held st), p 1, k 2 b, repeat from * around.

Rnd 3: * K 1 b, p 2, cable 2 knit back (place the first st on holder, hold in back, knit through back of the next st, knit through back of held st), p 2, k 1 b, p 1, repeat from * around.

Rnd 4: * K 1 b, p 1, cable back, cable front, p 1, k 2 b, repeat from * around.

Rnd 5: * K 1 b, p 1, k 1 b, p 2, k 1 b, p 1, k 1 b, p 1, repeat from * around.

Heel. Divide the sts so that the top of the foot has 21 sts (two cable patterns and the 3-st column of twisted knit sts at each edge). The heel is worked back and forth in stockinette st on the remaining 15 sts, always slipping the first st of each row. On the first row, decrease down to 13 sts by knitting 2 together centered over each of the two cable patterns (to make up for 2 of the increased sts when you started the cable pattern). Work the 13 heel sts for 4 more rows, ending with a knit row.

The heel is turned in just six rows.

← We're sure you've got a tiny ball of special, fine yarn lying around somewhere, waiting for a project. Here it is. This stocking requires a certain amount of knitting finesse, but it goes very quickly because there aren't many stitches! Follow Mary Spanos' directions and hints, and you'll find yourself making these in a lot of odd moments. They're big enough to fit a special present into . . . although this photo is "bigger than life."

Row 1: P 6, p 2 tog, p 1, turn. *Row 2:* Sl 1, k 1, k 2 tog, k 1, turn. *Row 3:* Sl 1, p 2, p 2 tog, p 1, turn. *Row 4:* Sl 1, k 3, k 2 tog, k 1, turn. *Row 5:* Sl 1, p 4, p 2 tog, p 1, turn. *Row 6:* Sl 1, k 5, k 2 tog (7 sts remain).

Instep and foot. Pick up 3 sts along the left side of the heel flap, work across the 21 sts in pattern for the top of the foot, pick up 3 sts along the right side of the heel flap, work across the 7 heel sts. Decrease the instep sts (those you just picked up along the sides of the heel flap) by working an ssk on the right instep and k 2 tog on the left instep every other rnd twice (30 sts remain). Continue working on 30 sts until there are 8 twists in the cable pattern, ending with rnd 3.

Toe. Divide the sts so that there are 15 sts for the top of the toe, 13 sts for the bottom of the toe, and 1 st on each side as a seam st. Immediately decrease 2 sts on the top of the toe by k 2 tog centered over each of the two remaining cable patterns. Shape the toe by working ssk on the right side of each seam st and k 2 tog on the left side of each seam st (4 sts decreased) every other rnd until 8 sts remain. On the next decrease rnd, decrease down to 4 sts as follows: * Slip 2 knitwise, k 1, pass both slipped sts over, k 1, repeat from *.

Finishing. Break the yarn, and using a small tapestry needle, thread the yarn through the remaining sts, draw it tight, and secure it to the inside of the stocking. Work any other ends into the inside. Wash and block the stocking. Sew on a ribbon for hanging.

Mary Spanos is a programmer for Southern Bell Telephone company. She spins and knits heirloom-quality projects (we said that, not Mary). She likes to use natural-colored wool from a special flock in Alabama tended by her friend Pia Cusick.

This is the actual size of Mary's stocking.

There's lots of air in this yarn.

Bibliography

Bernat's On Your Toes! Handicrafter No. 218. Uxbridge, Massachusetts: Emile Bernat and Sons, 1975.

Bush, Nancy. "Hose." *Knitter's* 5, no. 4 (Issue 13, Winter 1988): pages 16–18.

Don, Sarah. *Fair Isle Knitting.* New York: St. Martin's, 1979.

Duncan, Ida Riley. *The Complete Book of Progressive Knitting.* New York and London: Liveright, 1968.

Hansen, Robin, and Janetta Dexter. *Flying Geese and Partridge Feet: Traditional Mittens from Up North and Down East.* Camden, Maine: Down East, 1986.

Harrell, Betsy. *Anatolian Knitting Designs.* Istanbul, Turkey: Redhouse Press, 1981.

Knitter's (Summer 1992). Focus on entrelac knitting.

Ligon, Linda. *Homespun, Handknit.* Loveland, Colorado: Interweave Press, 1987.

Menz, Deb. " 'Multi-step' Carding." *Spin·Off* 14, no. 4 (Winter 1990): pages 46–48.

_____. "Using Lanaset Dyes on Fibers." *Spin·Off* 15, no. 4 (Winter 1991): pages 52–59.

Mon Tricot's 1300 Pattern Stitches. Paris: Mon Tricot, 1981.

Mon Tricot Knitting Dictionary: Stitches and Patterns. Paris: Mon Tricot, n.d.

Vogue Knitting (Winter 1991–'92). Focus on entrelac knitting.

Walker, Barbara G. *The Craft of Lace Knitting.* New York: Charles Scribner's Sons, 1971.

Walrath, Gerry Kay, and Marge Ferrin. "Kool-Aid Dyeing." *Spin·Off* 12, no. 2 (Summer 1988): pages 41–43.

Zilboorg, Anna. "Turkish Knitted Stockings." *PieceWork* 1, no. 2 (September/October 1993): pages 54–63.

Zimmermann, Elizabeth. *Knitting Without Tears.* New York: Charles Scribner's Sons, 1971.

Suppliers

Check your local stores for interesting ideas and tools, and ask them to stock what you need. But if you can't find the right stuff, discover the world of mail order. Here are some resources to start with:

Custom Colors, 4743 Balsam Street, Las Vegas, Nevada 89108. Phone or fax: (702) 645-4227. Orders: (800) 347-4228. *This is where Barbara Evans got her Hott Soxx batts to spin.*

Fingerlakes Woolen Mills, Stewarts' Corners Road, Genoa, New York 13071. (800) 441-9665, ext. 4. *The roving we used when testing Hannelore Krieger's fleece-lined socks came from here.*

Louët Sales, PO Box 267, Ogdensburg, New York 13669. (613) 925-4502. *Garry Aney's Coopworth roving came from Louët's ample stock of spinning fibers.*

Patternworks, Box 1690, Poughkeepsie, New York 12601-0690. Customer service: (914) 462-8000. Fax: (914) 462-8074. Orders: (800) 438-5464. *Having trouble finding double-pointed needles, 11-inch circular needles, and good, commercially spun yarns? This is a place to look.*

Ruth's Wheel of Fortune, RD 1, Box 389, Warner, New Hampshire 03278. (603) 456-3653. *This is the source for the "Crayola" hand-painted Romney roving which Claire Ottman used to make her cabled sweat socks.*

Schoolhouse Press, 6899 Cary Bluff, Pittsville, Wisconsin 54466. (715) 884-2799. *A broad range of needles, basic and loveable (usually all wool) yarns, and unusual books, including a few treasures on socks. . . .*

For information on handspinning books and *Spin-Off* magazine, contact **Interweave Press,** 201 E. Fourth St., Loveland, Colorado 80537-5655. (970) 669-7672

Index

Abbreviations and techniques are on pages 17–19. An overview of socks by designer, yarn size, and gauge is on page 41.

acrylic/cotton 26
Alexander, Kathryn 7
alterations 5
Anatolian stockings 15
Aney, Garry 30
angora 23, 51
angora/Merino 20
angora/Rambouillet 26
arrow-patterned socks 11
Atkins, Susan 44
backward loop cast-on 17
basic socks 51
Blazenko, Ruth 51
blue-and-white socks 48
cable cast-on 17
cabled sweat socks 29
cast-on, backward loop 17
cast-on, cable 17
Christmas stocking ornament 53
circular needles 5, 55
commercial yarn 5
Coopworth 30, 55
Corriedale 30, 39
cotton/acrylic 26
crochet, reverse single 18
crochet, single 17
Cushing dyes 39
Daurelle, Jude 39
diamond socks 33
Dibelka, Wilma 48
difficulty 5
Dolson, Ellen 15
double knitting 13
double-knit socks 13, 20

dyes 30, 39, 51
easy socks 22, 30, 47
entrelac socks 7
equipment 5, 55
Evans, Barbara 42
Fair Isle socks 35
felted socks 44
fireside socks 47
fitting 5
fleece-lined socks 23, 55
Fouquette, Robin 26
fundamental socks 39
gauge 5, 41
"girly girl" socks 26
Gooth-Buchanan, Joan 47
heavy socks 22
hiking boot socks 38
hot sox 44
Hott Soxx batts 42, 55
hound's-tooth socks 33
instep gusset 5
Jaeger, Margaret 35, 38
kid mohair 15, 20
knee socks 35, 42
Kool-Aid dyes 51
Krieger, Hannelore 23
lacy socks 11, 26
Lanaset dyes 30
Lincoln 15, 39
luxury yarns 53
Macrae, Irene 22
Menz, Deb 30
Merino 42
Merino/angora 20
Merino/silk 11
mohair, kid 15, 20
needles 5
nylon 39, 42

odds and ends 47
ornament stocking 53
Ottman, Claire 29
overviews of socks 41
parts of a sock 5
pencil pouch 5
quantities of yarn 5
Rambouillet 23
Rambouillet/angora 26
Rather, Marty 33
reinforced socks 39
reverse single crochet 18
rib stitch, modified 42
rib socks 30
Romney 29, 38, 39, 55
shaped toes 33
Sherman, Jean 11
silk 51
silk/Merino 11
single crochet 17
single crochet, reverse 18
size, checking 5
Slemko, Val 20
sock, parts of 5
socks, easy 22, 30, 47
Southdown 15
Spanos, Mary 53
spiral rib socks 30
stocking ornament 53
sweat socks 29
techniques 17–19
three-color knee socks 42
Tibetan socks 6, 7
toes, shaped 33
Turkish stockings 15
Varney, Diane 7
Wright, Jean 13
yarn 5, 32, 41

These are some of our test socks, worked in commercial yarns.